TRUE STORIES & PRACTICAL LESSONS
FOR YOUR JOURNEY

ANGELA THOMAS

THOMAS NELSON
Since 1798

NASHVILLE   DALLAS   MEXICO CITY   RIO DE JANEIRO   BEIJING

Published in Nashville, Tennessee. Thomas Nelson is a trademark of Thomas Nelson, Inc.

Thomas Nelson, Inc. titles may be purchased in bulk for educational, business, fund-raising, or sales promotional use. For information, please e-mail SpecialMarkets@ThomasNelson.com.

Library of Congress Cataloging-in-Publication Data
Thomas, Angela, 1962-
  Single mom life : true stories and practical lessons for your journey / by Angela Thomas.
    p. cm.
ISBN-10: 0-7852-2128-X (hardcover)
ISBN-13: 978-0-7852-2128-9 (hardcover)
ISBN-10: 0-7852-8912-7 (IE)
ISBN-13: 978-0-7852-8912-8 (IE)
  1. Single mothers--Religious life. 2. Christian women--Religious life. I. Title.
BV4529.18.T45 2007
248.8'431--dc22

                                                                              2007004623

Printed in the United States of America
07 08 09 10 QWM 5 4 3 2 1

For Lisa

Your organization and servant heart
are such selfless gifts of love.

Thank you for helping us
hold this crazy life together
every single day.

contents

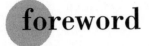# foreword

My mother made me play the Tuba because Tubas were provided by the school, and all the other instruments cost money. I did not want to play the Tuba because I was fat. I knew, even in the sixth grade, that being fat and playing the Tuba would reinforce a stereotype. My father, who left when I was a kid, was a basketball coach, and I suppose if he would have stayed I would have been a basketball player. There are no stereotypes about fat basketball players. I could have been the guy who only played defense, just standing around beneath the rim causing trouble in the paint. But my father was not around, so I played the Tuba. I thought at the time my life was being ruined, but it was not. I came to find out that hours of practicing the tuba made you a good kisser. Basketball does not make you a good kisser. Although it increases your chances of actually kissing anybody, it does nothing to tenderize your lips. All that to say I am a very good kisser. I didn't want to play the tuba, but now I am grateful.

My mother made my sister and me go to church. Because of this, I did not get to watch football on television. I am older now and don't live at home so I watch a great deal of football on television. I only go to church half the Sundays during football season, partly because I love football, and partly to express my independence from my mother. It's not a resentment thing, it's an independence thing. If I would have been raised by monkeys I would not eat bananas on Sunday. If you are judging me for only going to church half the Sundays during football season, then you are a pessimist. I *do* go to church the other half. And at church I learn about God, and sing about Him and pray to Him and take the Eucharist to remember Him. I do this because my mother made my sister and me go to church. I never wanted to go to church, but now I am grateful.

I was in Scotland earlier this year and some friends and I went on a hike in the Highlands. I learned about sheep there. There were a man and a dog in a meadow herding sheep across a creek, and my friend and I sat on a hill and looked down on the shepherd, and I couldn't help but think about Jesus' sayings that the church was like family and the church was like a flock of sheep. If this is the case, then churches and families are messier than you imagine. Sometimes we are lead to believe families and churches are to be clean, and children and sheep are supposed to line up in a straight row and go exactly where the Shepherd tells them to go. But this is not so. And anybody who disagrees has never raised children or shepherded sheep. Shepherding, along with raising children, looks precisely like an extended mental breakdown. Cast the image of the gentle shepherd walking through the green meadow aside as pure Hollywood.

I think the hardest job in the world is to be a single mom. The single mom makes decisions and wonders whether her decisions are right because she doesn't have somebody else to blame for the chaos. But God brings us chaos to teach us our lack, and to graciously guide us to Him for comfort and direction. What I have learned is that if there is love and if there is God then, somehow, the sheep make it to greener pastures. This isn't to say there is no better way, because there is, it is only to say that the world is fallen, and shepherding is messy, and there are pros and cons of being a basketball player just as there are with being a tuba player.

I am grateful to my friend Angela Thomas for boldly telling her story. I found my mom in these beautiful pages, and while I do wish I had a father growing up, I am also grateful for the shepherd God gave me. She knew that God could make up for any lack, and she is my hero.

All the counsel of God to you as you cross creeks and chose free tubas over basketballs. And all the comfort of God to you in your moments of desperation and confusion. One day your children will meet their father in the Eucharist and they will have you to thank. And if your children are very lucky, they will turn out to be great kissers.

Sincerely,
Donald Miller

P.S. Three last things: If you are raising sons, I think it is a good idea to let them watch football a few Sunday mornings out of the year. And I also think it is okay to let them date at a very early age. And to eat ice cream just before bed. Angela left these important things out, and I am not sure why. You see, God is already providing direction.

P.S.S. When your sons grow up, tell them to send me twenty bucks.

introduction

dear mom like me

Dear mom like me,

I am absolutely sure this is not how it should be. The more years go by, the more I am convinced that my kids would do better with their mom and dad loving each other and loving them and all living in the same house together. But that is not my story, nor will it ever be, and so the question has become, how will this single mom live?

It has taken me a while to get to the answers. And in many ways, my children and I are still tripping through the process, trying to find our way. But what I can tell you is that I have the best life I have ever known. No really, I actually do. My heart is becoming more and more healthy. My home is peaceful. My kids are the regular—silly sometimes, dorky others—kind of kids. I bless God because they are turning out to be wonderful, compassionate, very fun people, and I adore them.

As I began to write this book, I knew immediately that I wanted it to be encouraging, positive, funny, and full of hope and inspiration. That's the kind of book I'd like to read about life as a single mom. But I also knew that I had to tell the truth of my journey, which means beginning with the darkness and the pain. Perhaps a wonderful life is more valuable when the lessons to acquire it are hard fought, and the journey is many days that feel like two steps forward and fourteen steps back.

There is a chance that you picked up this book and you're not even a single mom. I am hoping that the stories of my journey will be valuable to you as well. May you find healing and rest in these lessons even if my path has been different than your own. And then one day, maybe you'll sit beside a single mom at a soccer game, and your words to her will be tender and blessed because you have glimpsed her life through mine. If you do, be sure to tell her that she's beautiful.

I'm obviously writing to single moms because that is my journey. But I'm hoping if a single dad picks up these words, there will be something here that connects in a healing, hopeful kind of way. Press on superdad. May you find new strength and vision for every challenge you face.

My last six years, wrapped in a whirlwind of emotion and activity, have been the most difficult yet the most rewarding I have ever known. Loving four children through their crazy lives, providing for us all, managing a home, and thinking about caring for myself feels a little like running the whole, wide world. Many of you know that.

But in these years, God has given me a passionate pursuit. I want to live an amazing life, even while raising these four kids alone. I don't want to wait until they are grown to become the best version of me. I want them to have that kind of mom *now*. They deserve the very best version of family that I can wrap a house around.

What if they could see in me *no* bitterness, ongoing healing, and a God-sized restoration? What if our home was the hub of activity for their friends? And we had parties and asked people over for dinner and invited the visiting missionary to stay in our spare room? What if we just acted like we're *normal* instead of focusing on what we're not? I think that a mom with a passionate, amazing life might just be the best foundation for kids to grow up healthy, educated, and wise.

Sometimes when I tell someone I'm a single mom, he or she looks at me like I am crippled. Single moms do have a triple-sized job. It feels like we live at warp speed, multitasking and spinning all the plates that get thrown at us. The responsibility of raising children well is enormous, and I don't think anyone should ever have to carry all of this alone. But we are not crippled. We're just single moms making our way in a couples' world.

Last Christmas Eve the kids were supposed to be with their dad, but it turned out that they were able to spend a few hours with me that night. You understand what a gift that was. We all went together to our church's Christmas Eve service, and I was just so grateful to not have to go by myself and sit there alone. The church was packed as the five of us filed into a row. I was happy and counting my blessings.

Then I made the mistake of looking around. All the other families seemed to be a man and a woman with some kids.

Whole families. In truth, many could have been third marriages, with blended kids, and dysfunctional as heck, but that night—at least in the glow of Christmas candles—they looked whole. I know there are other single moms at my church, but at that service I couldn't spot anyone who looked like us. And my heart ached.

Never mind what kind of families they are in private; the families with a man in their pew look put together, and we are so obviously single. Many days the ache of that unfair comparison won't seem to go away. And being a single-mom family can make us feel that we're relegated to live a second-class life. Crippled. Limping. Just doing the best we can with the scraps that remain. Many times I feel the ache, but I refuse to live like a crippled woman. I am a single mom. My children and I have been through it. But we've also been blessed beyond reason. I am choosing to live in the blessing.

I want you to understand and believe and desire that your life —yep, your single-mom life—can become a very amazing life. Our kids can rock the world, complete with tender hearts from emotional lessons learned early enough to give them a head start. You already know that being a single mom is the hardest job on the planet. We do more than anyone will probably *ever* appreciate or notice. The exhaustion that goes with this gig is nearly indescribable. But it can be done. A single mom with a houseful of kids *can* live a very beautiful life.

I am praying for you right now.

May you be encouraged. May you find healing and strength for the journey. May God pull you into His arms and hold you closer than you've ever known. A long, hold-you-tight, divine hug for a weary mom. And as God comes near, I pray you will move toward Him with fresh eyes to see His glory. A fresh heart to receive His goodness.

And I pray for those kids. Oh Father, You will have to cover them and protect them and provide for them. Our kids will become remarkable people because You have held them in your strong hands. Because You guide them and keep them from harm. So heal every wound and give them hearts of joy.

May the words of this psalm give you rest:

I look to the hills!
   Where will I find help?
It will come from the LORD,
   who created the heavens
   and the earth.
The LORD is your protector,
   and he won't go to sleep
   or let you stumble.
The protector of Israel
   doesn't doze
   or ever get drowsy.
The LORD is your protector,
   there at your right side
   to shade you from the sun.
You won't be harmed
   by the sun during the day
   or by the moon at night.

> The LORD will protect you
> and keep you safe
> from all dangers.
> The LORD will protect you
> now and always
> wherever you go.
> (Psalm 121 CEV)
> Amen.

It is such a privilege to walk alongside you with these words. Press on, my friend. God is for you. The hard days will not overtake you. As a gift to our children, we can become healthy moms who are strong and amazing women, in spite of our circumstances. There is a great, big life still in front of you.

Hug the pumpkins for me.

With love and tenderness,

Angela
Knoxville, Tennessee
Summer 2006

1

starting at zero

"I was wondering if you buy diamonds?" I whispered to the clerk, hanging my head in embarrassment and self-imposed shame.

"Just a minute and I'll get the owner," she offered.

While I stood there waiting, with just about my only worldly possession in my coat pocket, I watched a man choose a diamond three times the size of the one I wanted to sell. He had been meticulous with his research and obviously knew all the important features of an investment diamond. With the help of a clerk, he examined the one he had chosen closely and twice took it outside into the light to consider all of its properties. He talked some about clarity and color and flaws, but mostly he talked about how much he loved the woman he was buying it for. I stood in the corner and pondered the irony. This was his beginning and, on the very same day, my ending. He was full of enthusiasm and starry-eyed plans for a proposal. I was as empty as I had ever been, trying to feel as little as possible just so I could stand there and breathe in, breathe out.

So I watched him for a long time as I prayed for the courage to show my little diamond to whoever appeared, and then to have the nerve to ask him to buy it.

Eventually a small, busy man came through the back door. He seemed genuinely immersed in the details of jewelry being shown and overseeing the transactions of the clerks as he walked toward me. Our eyes met, and I knew that he knew. His countenance softened, and I could feel the instant tears trickle down my face when he asked how he could help.

Somehow I choked out that I wanted to sell my diamond. And that gracious man began to treat me like I had just offered him a bargain on the Taj Mahal. No shame. No judgment. Just one used diamond being sold in a business transaction. He pretended not to notice my tears. I'm so grateful he treated me like that.

In about thirty minutes he handed me a check for fourteen hundred dollars, shaking my hand and telling me ever so sincerely that he was sorry. I drove straight to the bank, cashed the check, and then walked two doors down to a furniture store. There I spent every dime of that money on beds for the children. Somehow it seemed OK to sell my engagement ring if the money was spent solely for them.

That day I started at zero. And I think that day was the beginning of our surviving.

My life as a single mom did not begin with surviving. So

I'll go back and tell you what happened at the beginning, or maybe it was the ending that actually became the beginning. Either way, I didn't do whatever it was very well.

becoming a single mom

The day my marriage was finally all over, I walked from room to room, nauseated, physically shaking, wiping tears, and packing three laundry baskets with whatever children's clothes I could find. I strapped two kids into their car seats, picked up the other two at school, and drove an hour to my parents' house. Mama made dinner, and my kids thought it was just a fun sleepover—except we slept over for three months. I realize it's exactly the opposite of how things usually go, but I never went back to live in the house with my things. The kids went every other weekend.

From that day until now I have been a single mom. I've done a hundred things wrong and finally gotten a few things right, but whichever way, I am absolutely sure this has to be the hardest job anyone could ever have. There should be a special medal for single moms. We should all get medals made of gold, with bouquets of flowers, for living this life and doing it with poise. Someone should stand and cheer every time we get the kids to school on time, fed and with clothes on. Or put stars on our single-mom charts for making it to the soccer games and school plays and for staying up late to talk to the kid who finally opened up. There should be a finish line to run through at the end of every day's marathon, corks popping from the celebratory champagne, a marching band playing

"There she is, Ms. Amazing Mom." And there should be someone to hold us tight because we've given all we had to give.

No one ever prepares to raise children alone. I had never even considered it an option, but there I was, fresh out of divorce court with a parenting plan and four heartbroken kids who had me for a mom.

Honestly, I'm not really sure how I made it through my first year of being a single mom. I look back now and know that a survival instinct kicked in eventually. Unfortunately, the will to keep going took a while to materialize. For the first few months, there were no living instincts inside of me at all. Just the desire to evaporate.

I know it was October. I'm sure it was a beautiful autumn in the mountains where I was staying. But all I can remember are the colors of my bedroom in the basement of my parents' house. Mostly taupe: taupe walls, taupe carpet. A peach bedspread, a peach headboard. A green lamp. A floral chair. Quite pretty, if you can see pretty. But I couldn't see pretty back then. Just blurry, colored shapes, with darkness closing in. I spent the days moving around in my room, but mostly I just lay on the bed and cried for all those months.

I look back now and realize that even that was a gift. Not everyone can take three months just to fall apart. I screamed for my children and the label they would now wear because of me: *You know their parents are divorced.* I pounded my pillow and yelled at the future they'd just been handed. Packing an overnight bag every other weekend. Divided affection. Deciding which parent to sit with at the school play. Dumb things like leaving a baseball jersey at one house when it's needed at the other. Opening presents on Christmas Day with one parent, and then leaving for a week at 3 p.m. *What in the world has happened?* I thought.

My hair was falling out. My eyes twitched. I lost about thirty pounds on the divorce diet. I was severely depressed, with all the classic symptoms. My parents were devastated and worried sick about their daughter, so they sent me to their family doctor. His nurse took my medical history and then used a stethoscope to listen to my broken heart. I left with a prescription to ease the depression, but I never went to the pharmacy for the medicine. For some weird reason, I wanted to learn from the pain.

In the time we lived with my parents, I was a mess. I would get up in the mornings, drive the children fifty minutes to school, drive back to my parents' house, go downstairs to my bedroom, and lie on the bed until it was time to pick them up again. God bless my mom and dad. They truly carried me through every single day. Mama cooked dinner and helped keep the clothes clean. They both listened to me talk about the same things night after night and left me alone when I couldn't say any more. I think my divorce is one of the most tragic things our family has ever been through, and I hated doing that to them. I still hate the tidal waves of pain it has caused so many people in my life.

As the months went by, I knew I had to do something about where to live, but I didn't have the energy to pursue it. And besides, I had nothing. Really and truly nothing. No furniture. No dishes. No towels. Nothing you would need to make a home. Still, a thirty-nine-year-old woman can live with her kids at her parents' house for only so long. I began to pray.

My girlfriend Lisa, as usual, began to do something. A friend of a friend, who was also a single mom, had pieced together secondhand furnishings after her divorce. Now she was getting remarried to a man who had a beautiful home, so she didn't need most of the things she had acquired. She wanted to leave them in the house she had been renting. Enter my friend Lisa, the woman who gets things done. She decided it would be the perfect place for me—her pitiful girlfriend, who had four kids and no place to live—and called to tell me so. "I don't know . . ." I said. "Maybe I'm not ready to do this." In case no one had noticed, I had no possessions, no job, and a big, fat mess of a life. I had no idea how I would pay the rent on a house. Lisa listened for a minute and then told me to meet her at the house at three thirty.

"Can we do it tomorrow?" I asked. She insisted that we do it *that day*. When you can't even put coherent sentences together, a bossy friend is a blessing.

Lisa was waiting when I drove up that afternoon with my carload of kids. There was a basketball goal at the end of the driveway, and my boys high-fived each other. All the kids ran around back and found two tire swings hanging from a 150-year-old tree. I walked through the garage into the tiniest kitchen I have ever seen and knew immediately that the five of us were supposed to live there. But how? I still didn't know what the rent was going to be and couldn't imagine being able to afford whatever it was.

I had figured out about how much money I thought I could make piecing together a couple of different jobs I hoped would come through. Turns out that the owner of the house

my single mom life

has one of the biggest hearts known to mankind, and renting the house was going to cost about the same as an apartment. So we set a move-in date, and I began to pray for enough work to take care of us and pay the bills.

Talk about walking by faith. I was physically healthy, and I promised God that I would do anything I had to do to provide for us. But when we moved into that house, I was completely in the dark about what that would be. The only plan I had was to work hard and live with integrity. There seemed to be only enough light for that one decision. From there the way wasn't clear. It was one baby step at a time.

The first baby step I took was the day I sold my diamond. The day I sold the only thing I had, to take care of the kids, was also the day I knew we were going to make it. There is something about walking through embarrassment and even the pangs of perceived judgment that makes you stronger. You begin to realize that courage doesn't kick in until you stand face-to-face with what you most feared. I began to know the strength of a faith I had only talked about but had never been forced to live.

When the kids' beds were delivered to the rental house, I remember thinking, *We have a roof, and we have beds. It's going to be OK.* But sheets. I had forgotten sheets. Then I opened the linen closet in the upstairs hallway. Sheets, towels, blankets, *everything* a mom could need to keep her kids warm. In the kitchen were dishes, utensils, and pots and pans. In the utility room sat an iron and ironing board. In the garage was a lawn mower. I had no idea the woman who moved out would leave so much. That day I began to call my house *The Blessing*. People would come over, and I'd ask, "Would you like me to show you around *The Blessing*?"

Becoming a single mom was the hardest thing that ever happened to me. The circumstances surrounding the decision were beyond devastating. The emotional toll it took on all of us was awful. I tell everyone who asks me for advice, "If there is any possible way on the planet to stay married, then stay married." I can't stand the thought of anyone going through that kind of pain. Divorce hurts everybody—I mean *every*body—and I never wanted to hurt anyone, especially not the beautiful children I love.

"it will never happen to me"

Becoming a single mother, well, it was *never*—and I mean *never*—going to happen to a girl like me, at least not through divorce. I am the daughter of Joe and Novie. They have been married, at this writing, for forty-five years. They are crazy in love, and, truly, I have never, ever heard them argue or seen them fight. We lived in the "happy house," which has its own weird set of dysfunctions that I'll save for another book, but *divorce* was a completely foreign word to our family. Most of my aunts, uncles, and cousins are still married to the ones they began with. And growing up, I didn't even know any divorced people or live on their street or go to church with them. So I grew up thinking I'd get married, live, and die with the man I chose. No options allowed, especially for nice Southern girls who love God.

After college, I did my graduate work at Dallas Theological

Seminary, where I mostly studied Bible and theology. I absolutely loved my years there. I loved the professors, the commitment among the student body and faculty to live with integrity and passion, and the melting pot of culture and ministries from around the world. Sometimes I tell people that I have a master's degree in "not getting divorced." I know what I was taught, not only in seminary but by my parents and all the people who have been a part of shaping my spiritual training through the years. Not only did they teach me well, but I also made a deep personal commitment to adhere to the promises I had made to marriage. So you see, though more than half the population will find themselves in a marriage that ends in divorce, it wasn't ever going to happen to me. I was prepared. I knew better. I could withstand anything with all my big-shot resolve. I was committed.

Then I was divorced.

I couldn't have predicted how the perfect life I had planned would explode, and I wouldn't have believed it if God Himself had sent me a letter telling me so.

Almost every divorced woman I've met says the same thing: this was *not* going to happen to her. Not many of us meant to end up as single moms. It wasn't the dream we had as little girls or teenagers or college grads with five-year plans. But divorce happens, and when it does, it leaves you crying in the dark and screaming out to God, *"How could this happen to me?"* Even grown women from single-parent homes often thought their determination and better choosing would keep their marriages from the same tragic ending. These women had lived through it as kids, and they weren't ever going to let that happen to their own children. But we all know now that there is the life you dream of, and then there is the one you actually live. Divorce makes my stomach hurt.

I realize that many of you became single moms for entirely different reasons. Two of my friends recently lost their husbands to tragic deaths. In an instant these women became the only remaining parent in each of their homes. Another friend's husband just succumbed to illness. My heart grieves with you if you have suddenly found yourself widowed. I won't even pretend to know how you feel or to understand the emotions you face. But I can still stand with you. As dark as it may be for you, this truth remains: there are children to be raised and a life, your life, still to be lived.

A couple of my never-married girlfriends have unselfishly adopted some of the most beautiful children on the planet. They knew what they were doing. They weighed the responsibilities with careful planning and prayer and then intentionally chose with their hearts. Though the risks would be great and the commitment was for a lifetime, my friends say they would make the same decision a million times over. Their kids are amazing, miraculously rescued from orphanages on the other side of the world. Yet none of my friends ever dreamed they would grow up and parent alone. But these moms also tell me that after you've done it alone, you understand why the best option is a mom and dad who love each other and raise the child as a team. It's painfully evident, even when a child is rescued, that his or her heart was made for both parents. One great parent is a gift from the hand of God. Two is the same gift multiplied. We all want that for our kids.

out of options, almost

No matter how we arrived in the Land of Single Mom, we're shocked at where we've wound up. The way I see it, it's not how it should be or how we *ever* wished to be, but, dang it all, this is how it is. We are single moms, and right from the start we have options:

WE CAN FALL DOWN, STAY THERE, AND JUST GIVE UP. Depending on how you became a single mom, an emotional falling down may be exactly how you responded to the circumstances that brought you here. To me that is exactly the right response, considering some of the stories I have been told. Who could even breathe after getting a text message saying your husband doesn't love you anymore? How could anyone even begin to process seeing a state trooper at the front door, hat in hand, bringing details of your worst nightmare come true?

When the life you had planned is suddenly and irrevocably taken from you, every soul fiber you have is entitled to scream in pain. No one should have to be strong enough to pretend to be courageous when ambushed by tragic loss. You should fall down in mourning and let your soul grieve the loss of what could—and should—have been. I told you about the months I lay in bed at my parents' house. I still can't imagine any other way to react to that kind of anxiety and pain.

So I believe falling down is legitimate. When everything falls apart, perhaps one of the healthiest things you and I can do is own the circumstances and grieve our loss, to cry aloud,

"It has all fallen apart, and I cannot possibly keep standing underneath all this heartache!" Grieve in whatever way gives your soul release. I call it falling down, but for you maybe it's hiding away or coming undone. Whatever we call it, we can't stay down or away or undone. We cannot give up. Life is calling our names. Amazing is waiting for you and for me. No matter how painful or extended your grief, a day will come when it's time to stand up again.

WE CAN GET UP, BUT STILL ALLOW OURSELVES TO BE BLOWN BY THE WINDS OF CIRCUMSTANCE, EMOTION, AND DISCOURAGEMENT. For a couple of years, this was me, standing as a single mom, yet uncertain and completely afraid. I let everyone else think for me and did whatever the next person suggested. Thankfully, those who loved me helped me make some great decisions during that time, but I felt so helpless and codependent. It was as if someone had to give me my next breath or I'd suffocate. If I didn't ask three people what to do, then I couldn't make a decision. I lived most of those days just reacting, going through the motions of being a mother. No real strength on the inside, just plodding along. I don't even know how my kids got fed and clothed those first years, but obviously they did, and, incredibly, I was the one who made it happen.

But standing and being blown about by each new dilemma and circumstance is not really living. That kind of life is insecure and fearful. You live without hope or expectation, unable to see what is possible for a woman like you with kids like yours. I want so much more for your single-mom life.

WE CAN STAND UP, SURVEY OUR WOUNDS AND OUR SURROUNDINGS, THEN DECIDE TO DO WHATEVER IT TAKES TO LIVE THE MOST AMAZING LIFE POSSIBLE. I realize it can take time to reach this decision and this kind of strong-woman resolve, but eventually it *will* be time. The grieving will be over. You will want to move on. The clouds that blocked your vision will begin to clear. There is a really good life waiting for you, and eventually it's time to do whatever it takes to live again. If I had read words like these before my heart could receive them, I'm sure I would have mumbled something like, "Impossible." Maybe you're not ready yet, but one day it will be time to get your life back. Your mind will clear, and you'll ask, "What will it take to begin living again?"

"What it takes" will be different for each of us, so take a look at the following and circle anything that could be a part of the next step for you:

- See a doctor about the depression that won't budge.

- Find out where the nearest recovery class is being held, and make plans to attend.

- Make time to sit down with your children and talk about where you all are and where you're going.

- Find a church where your family can be loved and embraced.

- Get away for a weekend, by yourself, to reflect.

- Enjoy a weekend of laughter with some girlfriends.

- Begin to journal your emotions and sort through your fears.

- Cry it out one more time.

- Decide that the crying is over and it's time to start anew.

It's up to you to find out what it will take to get on board the train to your new life. Some of you are ready, some are getting ready to be ready, and some are just surprised you're still breathing. But wherever you are on this journey, my prayers are with you. I believe with all my heart that God longs to hold you close, and He is able to provide for you, protect you, and heal all your brokenness. He is the only One who can take a single mom from zero to hope.

• • •

In each chapter I will share the same lessons God is still teaching me. You know, the growing-up stuff that life is made of.

A friend said to me, "It should encourage a lot of women that their single-mom lives aren't as awful as yours has been." We laughed about that, but I hope it's true. Some of your suffering, though, is greater than mine. On the other hand, some of you have been better protected and cared for. But for all of you, if I can offer any hope in these lessons, even the embarrassing ones, I will do so with honesty and candor. I'll own up to my stupid choices so you can avoid them. And as I write, I hope and pray that you and your beautiful children will be blessed beyond your understanding. I want you to live a passionate, fun-filled adventure. I know we thought it would be different, but here it is, and we can't afford to miss a thing. So here are my lessons for this chapter:

my lessons from starting at zero

GOD IS NEAR. When it was just the children and me, and I had no idea what the future held, a miraculous thing happened: I began to see God everywhere. I could finally hear His voice, because I became desperate for His instruction. Waiting with empty hands and kids to take care of, I was completely dependent on His provision. If God didn't come through, we would have nothing. I cried out for His compassion, begging many days, "Have mercy on us! Have mercy!" And God came with mercy. Even when I didn't *feel* mercy or God's presence at all, I look back and know that my prayers were being heard. I learned that neither feeling nor *not* feeling God determines His presence.

When I felt ashamed and unworthy of being cared for, our nearby God stooped down to pick me up and has carried me from zero to this very minute. Every lesson I have learned has been by His grace. Every ounce of strength and comfort has been given because of His promised faithfulness. He is more real to me now than ever before. God is near, and He takes care of women like us. And I tell you, He is good, very, very good.

In seminary, my favorite hymn was an old, beautiful song called "Great Is Thy Faithfulness." I used to stand in chapel, close my eyes, and sing all the verses as if I knew what they were talking about. Little did I know what a novice I was. As a single mom, the great faithfulness of God has been my salvation and strength. He has been near all along; but now when I sing about His faithfulness, I'm like a little girl, seated on her father's shoulders and crying out, "No one can get me now! I'm safe up here with my dad!"

YOU'RE GOING TO BE OKAY. When you are standing at zero, it's hard to believe and even harder to see, but I promise this: a woman who belongs to God and wraps herself in the truth of His goodness is going to make it.

As I began to experience more healing, I'd hear myself say, "It's going to be okay." My friends even gave me a T-shirt printed with those words so I could just point to my shirt. I had no firm answers for anything, but something on the inside was turning a corner. I began to hear God whisper, *I have you. It's going to be all right.* I can't tell you how ready I was to believe that.

Sometimes you just have to live as if you believe something is true until your experience proves it. I began to live as though everything would work out just fine. My kids were going to be okay. Our finances would be okay. My heart would even be okay. We didn't all have to be doomed to years of therapy and guilt and poor choices. Life could actually be amazing again.

THE KIDS WILL MAKE IT. Same song, second verse. Your kids live inside the shadow of what you are becoming. When you are going to be okay and you know it, that attitude transfers into their spirits. They will be okay too, because you are teaching them through your own bright countenance and choices.

my single mom life

GOING TO ZERO CAN MAKE YOU GRATEFUL AND GENEROUS. When you have nothing, absolutely *nothing*, then the fear of having nothing is taken away. You can learn a very powerful lesson from going to zero, having nothing, yet waking up with a tiny little dream still left in your heart. It is lovely to have nothing but live with kids who don't know it. Starting at zero can be one of the most beautiful gifts your character will ever be given.

At zero, everything you receive is a gift. The promise of work. Another week of groceries. A tank full of gas. A kind word from a stranger. An afternoon with the kids by someone's pool. Cut flowers for the table. Hot water for your shower. Everything makes you grateful, and you live grateful from encounter to encounter, because you have been to zero, and God has given you a new perspective. Life is more precious. People and their love for you become your blessings.

Zero also makes you generous. Once you have started over with nothing, you know what it feels like to receive goodness. So you give that same feeling to the next person, another mom or your kid's friend who is hurting and alone. A long hug. Room for another at dinner. A couch for someone to sleep on. You give and share what you have, because at zero it makes no sense to be stingy.

I have said this before, but I'll say it again: my brokenness, my going to zero, my losing almost everything, is the best thing I take into my future. I am a better woman because of it. I love more purely and without judgment. I live more passionately because zero has made me grateful.

Let zero make you gracious and thankful too.

• • •

A woman sells her diamond when she has run out of options. It's time to start over, and the grown-up, the person called Mom, has to do something brave.

Being a single mom might be a different path than the one you would have chosen. But now you're a single mom. Maybe you're afraid and stressed and so very tired of doing it all alone. This life is certainly challenging, and it's such a huge, hairy deal to have to begin again. But when you find yourself at zero, God is near. And the rest of your great, big life is all in front of you. Truth is, you and your kids are just getting started. So do whatever it takes and embrace the lessons as they come. We will become better women because of them. And I promise, the best is still to be.

2

a changed mom

My kids found an old family picture the other day. I was married at the time the picture had been taken. My youngest, AnnaGrace, looked about eight months old. It must have been Easter, because each child was dressed up, and the flowers in the background were in bloom. The kids were all so little in that picture. It was almost like a different family sitting on the rocks behind our old house.

Then one of my children asked, "Mom, who is that lady holding AnnaGrace?"

It was me.

I almost didn't recognize myself. Short, frumpy hair. Pup-tent dress. And the eyes! You'd think my eyes would always look the same, but this woman's eyes were empty. Sad. Lonely.

For a moment I actually wondered, *Who in the world* is *that?* But she had *my* teeth, and she was holding *my* kids. Yeah, it was me. I was embarrassed to see the woman I used to be.

Things have changed for me. But mostly it's about the eyes. Sure, they have a few more crow's feet. But the emptiness is gone.

How awful to have lived so empty for that long. How grateful I am to have been completely changed.

• • •

Sometimes, when I was empty, I would scream. And not muffled little screams either. The screaming that came ripping out of me was the real thing. I'm sure everyone inside (and probably outside) the house could hear me. I can't remember the last time it happened—certainly not in the last four years—but there was a season when, every once in a while, as everything caved in, I'd scream.

Sadly, the only people I ever screamed at were my children. Then, after screaming about whatever straw had just broken this camel's back, I would cry because of the terrified and wounded looks on my kids' faces. Sometimes I even saw fear. I am not a screamer, so I could tell my children didn't even know who I was when I let myself come unglued. Now I know that I screamed because I had nothing. Completely given out. An empty, desperate cry, kind of like a grieving. What an embarrassingly immature thing for such an educated woman to do in front of her children.

Today my kids refer to those screaming/crying episodes as "Mom's meltdowns." I have apologized. And they have forgiven me. They joke now about the occasional meltdown, but then their eyes say, *But don't ever do it again. We don't like "scary Mom."* No kid should have to endure "scary Mom." But mine did.

I don't know what you do when you're empty. Maybe you scream too. Maybe you cry or sleep or drink or make other poor choices. Perhaps you take it out on the children or make them suffer from your distance.

But you can't continue to live empty. It is the most lonely, desperate place in the world. And it hurts the people you love. And if you are empty, it's time for a change.

one big mess of a mom

When the kids and I moved into that first little rental house, I had no idea what was ahead for any of us. At first my time was spent just settling in and organizing our new home. I wanted to make it feel like home, so I painted the boys' tiny little bedroom and found some quilts they liked. The girls' room came together with new beds and donated chests of drawers. We refinished some of the furniture that had been left in the house. We hung posters and met the neighbors, and in just a short time, when we pulled into that driveway, we were "coming home."

Settling my family into The Blessing was a beginning step in our new life, but a bigger project lay ahead. That project was me. When you are a single mom, like it or not, you are the center of your family's little world. On any given day, our family functioned or did not function according to my strength— or lack thereof. If I was a mess, there was going to be a mess all the way around. If I was fun, guess what? We had fun.

At the beginning, I was such a roller coaster of emotion

and confusion. I tried to keep it from the children, but those kids can read their mama like a book. I'd hide out in my room when I felt the tears coming, but they knew. It was killing me that I was hurting them with my pain, and it quickly became obvious that it had to stop. If for no one else but the children, their mom had to get her life back or start a whole new one. To put it off would only mean more pain for all of us.

Maybe you've heard this about healing and recovery: *You have to choose to do it for yourself.* Well, *I* didn't—not for myself, that is. At that point, I was so beaten down and wounded that I could have just crawled into a cave, never to be seen again. But my kids needed a real, live mom. The kind of mom who smiles and means it. One who works puzzles and engages with more than an absent nod and an "Okay, honey." A mom who is dreaming again. Passionate again. Awake and alive and spilling over into their tender hearts. I decided to make it happen. My kids deserved that.

But God would have to take over. My broken-down heart needed a serious healing. I was a tangled mess, and I couldn't figure out how not to be a mess on my own.

the only one

When I became a single mother, a gazillion things changed. There was the immediate change in where we lived and how we survived, of course. But the emotional and spiritual trauma was the part that kept me a mess for way too long.

I am a woman of great faith. I know you don't know me, but I have loved God for a long time now. I've had Bible training and taught others from both my intellect about Him and my heart of passion for His ways. I have tried to live my life based on His principles and instruction. I believe in God as my Creator, and it makes sense to me that the Creator knows how this life should be lived. I believe God sent His Son, Jesus, to save me from the eternal penalty my sin has earned.

You'd think that a Jesus girl like me would instinctively know where to turn when her soul has become empty. I did know, but when I entered the Land of Single Mom, I felt that God was disappointed in me. According to some, He was even mad at me and probably didn't want anything to do with a woman who couldn't keep it together. And though I had always taught others about the forgiveness and mercy of our Father God, I held myself to a haughty, higher standard. I wanted to be perfect for God and keep my slate clean. So when my life blew apart, I hid, embarrassed to show God all my brokenness. Ashamed of my emptiness. Mad at myself because I knew better but couldn't *make* it better. I couldn't get it all cleaned up and perfect for God.

Single-mom articles encourage you to get out, meet people, take a class, improve your skills, or get away with your friends. All those things are incredibly valuable. I have taken the advice in many of the articles and done almost every moral thing suggested to improve my surroundings and contentment and inner peace. I've been on trips, gotten facials, tried new restaurants, stepped out of my comfort zone, met new and interesting people, and even taken a class or two. And all of that was fun and horizon expanding, but not one of these activities did squat for filling my empty soul. I'd drive home from a gallery opening, where I'd had intriguing conversations with unique, eclectic people, and my emptiness would greet me in the car. Ever present. The cup of my soul was still empty and dry.

I have been slow with God. Ridiculously slow. The first time I heard the truth of Jesus as Savior, it immediately resonated with my soul. I knew I needed Him, and right then, I fervently prayed and asked Him to save me. But the next time I heard the gospel, I prayed that again. I bet I asked Jesus to be my Savior 150 times between high school and college. Just to make sure. Always afraid I'd left something out. One more time for extra measure. I was never certain I'd done it exactly right. On top of that, I *was* certain I wasn't worthy, so I stayed off balance and without confidence. Oddly, I hoped God was pleased with my perpetual seeking.

I vividly remember the very last time I prayed and asked Jesus to become my Savior. That's when I heard God say to me, in my spirit, *Angela, you are wearing Me out. You never have to ask Me again. I heard you the first time.* The only One who has filled me completely is our Lord, God. And the only way He got me to come out of hiding was to come in and get me. Throughout the divorce, I prayed and worshipped and sought God for direction, but I hid my empty soul from Him because of my shame. I kept a cover on the deeper questions and ultimately, my fear of their answers.

Now, though, as a single mom, I was empty again. And slow again. It took me so long to finally whisper across the distance between us, "How could You ever love a woman like me? I know You must be disappointed. I imagine You're angry too. Is my life ugly to You? Do You think I'm beautiful?"[1]

Maybe my soul stayed empty for so long because I was

---

1. You can read about this whole journey in my book *Do You Think I'm Beautiful?*

still being slow. But finally, I heard God say to me, *Angela, I don't think you know your Bible very well, because if you did, then you'd know that Romans 8 says there is nothing*—nothing *that can come to you, nothing you can choose or suffer, no number of consequences you can bear, no victimization, no amount of abuse or poverty or brokenness or imperfection or demons or anything in all creation*—nothing *that can ever change My love for you* (from verses 38–39).

When I heard God that day, just that clear in my spirit, I wept. And God and I began to make an exchange that day. I held out my brokenness and shame; He replaced them with mercy and unending love. I showed Him my consequences; He exchanged them for forgiveness. I timidly revealed my fears, and the God of heaven bent down and pulled me to Himself. I saw myself in His arms, where no evil person or plot could touch me. I belonged to God.

My soul was finally being refilled. He still wanted me. Broken me. Imperfect me. Divorced, single-mom-with-four-kids, how-are-we-ever-going-to-do-this? me. The truth of His great, big love broke through. I had needed a Savior the first time, and He had never let go. Never turned His back. I was His, and He was mine. His was the love that would make me whole again. Coming to that personal understanding of God's devotion to me is the only thing that gave me courage to begin anew.

Maybe *you* need a Savior. God promises to come the first time you ask.

Maybe you want to know if God still wants anything to do with a woman like you. He wrote Romans 8:38–39 for you too.

Maybe you have a lot of heartache to exchange. That is the

beauty of redemption. God gives it freely to every one of us who will lay our shame, insecurity, and brokenness on His altar.

making a trade

Redemption is when you bring something of little value or which has become a liability, and an exchange is made for something better. You trade in your wounds or consequences for astounding, lovely blessings, in spite of the negative, or maybe even because of it. In the fullness of redemption, brokenness is mended by love. Aimless wandering becomes satisfied, visionary living. Lies are traded for truth. Mourning becomes dancing. A million broken pieces are rearranged into a vibrant, intact, beyond-your-wildest-dreams journey.

That kind of redeeming trade has happened for me. And the exchange just keeps going. The One who is making the trade, the Redeemer, is the One I call Perfect Love, God, the *only* One who can turn broken into beautiful. Apart from His faithfulness to me, there would have never been redemption. I am convinced that His mercy is the means by which my life began again. Without His precious love, I'm sure I'd be in an unmarked cave somewhere, probably all moldy by now and nearly blind from squinting in the dark. Instead, I am so incredibly grateful that God wouldn't let that happen, even to a woman like me. And what He has done for me, He is ready to do for you.

> *He redeemed my soul from going down to the pit,*
> *and I will live to enjoy the light.*
> (Job 33:28 NIV)

Have you held back with your soul? You've tried all the gimmicky, better-life strategies, but you still come up empty at the end of the day? Be honest with yourself and hold out that emptiness to God. He will exchange it for fullness.

If there were really any other way around the emptiness, I'm sure you would have discovered it by now. The only answer I have known for my empty soul is this big, deep, wide, and high love of God. Big enough for me and big enough for you.

I don't know if you need to begin again. Maybe you have already found your way into the amazing life that awaits you and your children. But maybe you stand among your million pieces, wondering what will become of you, asking how anything lovely could come of these circumstances. Where will you turn? What about the children? Maybe you are tired and you can't even muster up the energy to make dinner, much less think about beginning again.

If your spirit is broken and your body is weak and your children suffer because their mom is empty, I'm praying that something in these words will reach into your darkness. I know the One who will heal your broken heart. The One who promises a holy exchange. He is here. Our God is able to make you whole. You can begin your life again.

The holy exchange called redemption has changed my life completely. I began to live again when I started believing that God still had a miraculous life left for me. With every passionate bone inside of me, I believe that for you too.

I don't know if you need to stop for a few minutes and take a deep breath to let some of this settle into your heart.

Maybe you need to take a while to consider where you are

with God. Are you distant and empty, or are you filled and wrapped up in His arms? I have been both. Many times, my distance and emptiness are the very things that tell me I need God the most.

When I feel my mind rejecting spiritual thoughts and the pursuit of God, a warning flare shoots up that screams, *Angela, you are bad off!* I try to see that flare shoot up the first time and let it send me back into the arms of God.

Are you far away from God? Have you found yourself empty all over again? The emptiness will scream inside of you, sending up flares to tell you where you are right now.

Can you know God and still have pain or heartache that needs a righteous trade? I did. As I said, I have always believed in God, but I haven't always been honest with Him. Many times I have kept my distance when what I needed was to run to Him for healing and affection. And when we live with distance between us and God, we are out of sync, as if we are stuck or life has been put on hold. Do you know God, yet feel stuck? Then maybe there is *something* you need to trade, something you've been holding back until now.

What pieces of your life need to be redeemed? You can start with your heart or an attitude or a habit. The sooner you are honest with the One who already knows your need, the sooner the necessary life-giving change will begin.

Where do you need to hear God speaking clearly concerning your heart? If you were quiet and told God the truth, what would you hear Him saying to you? If you're hearing judgment, you are not hearing from God. The Bible says, "There *is* therefore now no condemnation to those who are in Christ Jesus"

my single mom life

(Rom. 8:1 NKJV). When you hear from God, He will be speaking in love, offering words of mercy and redemption. The condemning voice is that of the accuser, who wants you to keep living with an empty, broken heart.

Don't be slow with God. Right now, take whatever time you need, get down on your knees, and call on His strong name. Write it out if you can't speak it. But lay the truth on His altar. Persist with God. Don't let another empty day go by. God is waiting for you to trade your empty soul for the fullness He has promised.

Sometimes a relationship with God will sound like "pie in the sky" to the woman who is at zero. I get it. You might feel like this thing with God is too good to be true or that you've never experienced this kind of God-love before. Well, that's kind of the whole point with God. A new life for the hopeless. Healing instead of brokenness. Going beyond your imagination just as the last dream backed out the driveway. If you find yourself at zero and then you look up to God, you just might want to hang on. I have a feeling God's getting ready to show off. He's ready to demonstrate to the emptiest woman on the planet what God-change and God-love can look like for her.

lessons from a changed mom

SOUL EMPTINESS WILL HURT YOUR CHILDREN. When you parent your children from emptiness, they get little or none of the nurture and consistency they need from you. I don't say this to inflict more guilt, because Lord knows we all have enough. I just want to remind you that emptiness is unhealthy for you *and* the children. So, even if you aren't motivated to change for yourself, would you do it for your children? They deserve a shot at life with a healthy mom whose redeemed life is becoming amazing.

YOUR REDEMPTION WILL SHAPE THEIR SOULS, YOUR PARENTING, AND THE WAY YOUR CHILDREN LIVE THE REST OF THEIR LIVES. When the empty soul finds healing and begins to fill with the goodness of God's love, do you know what happens? It spills over. When you have been filled to all fullness by the living water that is Jesus, you start sloshing that Jesus water out all over the place—all over the children. Here's the way I think about it: I wonder how kids will turn out who have lived inside a healthy home. Not an unattainably perfect place, but a predominately happy home, a safe place where mistakes are forgiven, where you can be yourself and trust that there will consistently be acceptance and lavish love. A place where it's silly sometimes and serious others. How would it be to give my children that kind of a place to grow up? How will that affect their children? Their futures? Their homes and the futures that await them?

A home with one parent is not the path I had intended for my children, but the bigger question continues to be, how now shall we live? I want to become a woman with a changed life. A healthy heart. A full, alive, and passionate soul. If this happens for you, not only have you reaped the benefits personally, but your kids will get a head start, because they will have lived in a place where difficult circumstances became a really great life.

How cool will that life lesson be for them? I think it will serve to give them tools they'll need to overcome life's inevitable disappointments and failures. I think they will understand more about hope. I believe that if you live healthy in front of them, they might just grow up to become healthy, balanced adults who multiply and pass on the beauty of God's redemption.

What God does for us fills the emptiness so that we are able to give that same kind of selfless love to our children, our families, and the friends who walk alongside us. When I am full of the knowledge of God, made clean by His forgiveness, and walking in the grace He has given to me, then I am a really cool mom. I am not Supermom, but in that full place, I know that I am loving my children as they were made to be loved.

When I am full, I'm not wishy-washy about my role as protector or provider. I overlook the small things. I major on my kids' hearts and look into their eyes and hear what's on the inside of them, trying to get out. I am not whiny or grumbling. I forgive them even as I'm giving out consequences. I dance with them more and take longer to brush their hair or watch a new skateboard trick. I am peaceful because I am living from the gift of God's peace to me. I know they can feel the difference. I am not empty, and they are the benefactors.

God's grace flows freely from my heart into theirs. And we are better. And life is brighter. And hope abounds.

GOD IS NOT MAD AT YOU. A lot of people I meet believe that God is perpetually mad at them. So they are afraid to get too close to "the Angry One," who enjoys doling out punishment for every offense. And since there's almost nothing they can ever do to please Him anyway, they put off the needed exchange, because God is probably mad about it.

But would you send *your* only son to die for someone you just like a little? No! For goodness' sake, you'd only send him to die for those you can't bear to live for eternity without. The ones you are wildly in love with. For your beloved. For your baby girl. That's who God sent His only Son for.

God has known from the very beginning that you and I would need a Savior. He is well acquainted with our humanity. And He's *not mad about it*. We are the created, and He is the Creator. You need a Savior. I need a Savior. And I still need a Savior this very day to forgive me of my sins, to give guidance to my next decision, to parent these children well, and to work by the power of the Holy Spirit to change me from the woman I have been into a woman who looks more like Him.

What if it's true? What if God really isn't mad? What if He is tenderly waiting for you to come to Him? Then come.

Come empty; He fills to overflowing.

Come with liabilities; He already knows and wants you anyway.

Come broken; He is the healer.

Come embarrassed or lost or without hope. You need a Savior, and He has never been mad that you were made to need Him.

A WOMAN WITH A REDEEMED HEART BECOMES STRONGER, ABLE TO NAVIGATE THE CIRCUMSTANCES AND INEVITABLE CHALLENGES THIS LIFE BRINGS. I used to go down—I mean, crying jags and deep, prevailing sadness—

every time there was another single-mom challenge. I couldn't catch my breath. I'd pace around the house. Then I'd call twenty people to ask them what they thought I should do. I was an empty woman back then, still scurrying about, trying to piece my life back together on my own every time the next thing fell apart. When the heart is redeemed, you begin to see the good. No status symbol, like a big house or a diamond ring, makes life good; but with a changed heart, even if you're living just above the poverty line, you can wake up every morning and say to yourself, "My life is good."

God just keeps refilling and redeeming, and what is amazing to me is that you will become stronger. Just this weekend, I received voicemails and e-mails that brought difficulty to our family of five. We may have to go to court. The next few months could be hard and expensive. But my soul is full, and I am at peace. I remember all that God has already done for me. He'll do it again. We will walk through whatever comes. And I won't be dead on the other side. *This* mom has been filled by the powerful presence of God, and there is no going back.

• • •

If there was any way to hang a flashing neon banner over a chapter, I wish the publisher could do it to this one. You'd open the book and then—*bang!*—redemption truth would—*bling bling!*—grab your attention and take hold of your heart. I believe you are a mom who wants more. I think you desire the best version of you. A peaceful life. Great kids. Laughter. Contentment. A sweet fullness to savor.

That whole great-life-with-great-kids thing revolves around these redemptive truths. So this chapter is the hinge. The turning place. You can remain empty—been doing that for a while now—or you can choose God and His divine exchange. The pivotal choice is yours.

What will you do with your emptiness? What will happen to the kids if you don't change?

But a new mom with a new heart? Wow. Wouldn't it be something if God used all the things you are going through to make you better? And your kids slept every night in the same house with the *coolest* changed woman they've ever met?

3

hey there, lonely mom

Loneliness is the most terrible poverty.
—Mother Teresa

Two of my friends, who live in two different cities, called me on the same day and said exactly the same thing: "Angela, you have to go see the movie *Must Love Dogs*. It's about a lonely, recently divorced woman and all the ridiculous things she goes through with her family and dating. You're gonna laugh your head off. It's just hilarious!" One of my friends was so insistent that I see it that she said, "*Promise* me you will go tonight, and then call me as soon as you're out. I just can't wait to hear what you think."

So I called my neighbors, Lisa and Dave, told them I had been commanded to go see a movie that was going to make us laugh till we cried, and asked them to go with me. Right after dinner, we left all our kids at their house, with one or two older ones in charge, and headed off to what was supposed to be the funniest movie ever . . . for a woman like me.

The theater was packed that night, and we were thankful to get three seats together. In fact, there was one empty seat beside me, and the rest of our row was full. Just as the movie began, a man came working his way across Lisa and Dave and almost fell into the seat next to me. Lisa elbowed me in the side, and even in the dark I could feel her looking at me, like, *Hey, there's a man!* I told her to stop it. I didn't go to the movie looking for a man; I came to laugh, so let's get on with it.

I don't know if you saw this movie. If so, maybe you thought it was the funniest thing ever. But honestly, I can't recommend it to any of the single moms I know. I had come for a lighthearted chick-flick. And maybe it *was* funny. I heard everyone else in the theater cracking up. I even laughed—a couple of times. But that movie ended up being really hard for me.

There is one scene where the lead character, Sarah Nolan, played by Diane Lane, is in her empty kitchen. She is in rumpled clothes, no makeup, her hair is a mess, and she is standing against the stove, drinking a cup of coffee. She is alive and healthy, but obviously so very alone and depressed. The soundtrack comes up underneath the pitiful scene and begins to play that old '70s hit, "Hey There, Lonely Girl." Everyone in the theater lost it. I could hear them cackling over the music and the moment. And I knew in my head it was funny. But it hit so close to home that all I could do was cry. I mean, suck-it-in-so-they-won't-hear-me kind of cry.

By the time the whole thing was over, I was in a pit. This

movie was about a lonely woman with *no* kids. I was going home to my four pumpkins, thinking to myself, *It's funny if it's not you. And if you're a single mom, just multiply the lonely pain.* For months afterward I would sing out loud, "Hey there, lonely girl," trying to make myself laugh about it. But lonely just isn't that funny anymore.

• • •

I don't think other people believe that single moms are all that lonely. We've got kids who live with us, and those brilliant little minds are always coming up with a million things for us to do for them. And single moms are ridiculously busy, they reason, so how could we be lonely? We are balancing and multi-tasking more than any sane human being should have to. But maybe that in itself is a part of it. When you are holding up the world, all by yourself, fatigue sets in. Everyone assumes you can be strong because you are getting it all done, but no one *wants* to be that strong. And really, no one should have to be. Eventually the fatigue is overwhelming, and being tired just makes you lonelier.

Loneliness, maybe more than anything, has been my greatest struggle these past years. There have been a lot of other heart-wrenching struggles, but loneliness is the thread that has woven through everything. Honestly, not a day goes by, even the craziest, most productive and extraordinary ones, when my heart doesn't yearn for someone to share it with. God made each of us for companionship. Healthy, loving, nurturing companionship. And the person who tries to live as though that's not true is just pretending.

Some people act as if they don't need anyone. I think it's a front, a distancing technique to keep hurt away. I've acted like that when I was afraid of more pain. After you've been hurt in relationships more times than you can count, you begin to tell yourself you'd be better off alone. Of course, lonely is a million times better than lonely *and* living in misery. But just plain lonely still stinks. I'd love to live a few years without it.

Today is a typical day for me. I was up by five thirty to get the kids ready for school. Breakfast. Carpool. Quick stop back at home to put in another load of laundry. An hour at the gym. A run by Target for a Monday-morning restock on milk, bread, and the regular groceries. Back to the house and working at my computer by ten. It's a very fine day. No one is mad at me, as far as I know. The kids seem fine, and I am sitting in my little office, writing my heart out. I had a healthy homemade salad for lunch. I have answered all my e-mails. The load of towels is folded. It's a good, good life and a good, good day. But underneath every great thing that's going on for me is this weird, ever-present longing for more. A lonesomeness that comes with being a single mom in a couples' world. A single woman in a family of five.

Sometimes I see lonely coming and try to head it off at the pass. Like a few months ago, when Lisa invited me to the new small group they were starting at their house. Lisa and her husband, Dave, are some of my closest friends. I love them, and I know they love me. The small group would be composed of several couples from church. They planned to meet once a week for food and fellowship, and they had decided to study some books that I really enjoy. I truly like all of the people who were going to come, and I knew they would welcome me with open arms. And most of the time I'd rather be with other families and married friends, but committing to join a small group of couples just felt really lonely. I knew that if I went, I probably wouldn't open up and be honest. Just talking to Lisa about it made me want to cry.

"Angela, this is not going to be a marriage thing—more of a book club, with great discussion. You'll love it."

"I know I'd love being with you guys, but you'll all be there in your healthy marriage relationships, and then there'll be me. I'll try to hide my loneliness so you won't have to feel sorry for me. I'll be lively and intellectual and funny so the whole group won't have to see how much it aches for me to be alone. But then I'll walk home from your house, crying my eyes out. I don't think I can set myself up for that, week after week."

"You're kind of being a baby."

"I know, but I just can't come."

I do feel like a baby sometimes. Whiny. Emotional. Prone to tears. Trying not to let the lonely vibe out and ruin someone else's day. I'm sure the people in my life are over it. I mean, I've been singing this same tune for years now. And my friends have all gone beyond the rational concept of friendship and compassion. They stick around and listen, no matter what. But I am so weary of lonely. I'd truly love to move on or pretend it's gone or *anything* except acknowledge that, dang it, I'm still battling lonely. And if I'm tired of *being* lonely, I imagine they have to be tired of hearing about it.

Sometimes lonely has a way of sneaking up on you. For me, the weirdest things can make me feel all alone in my desire to love well and live an amazing life. Like when I take my kids to play putt-putt. We'll be having a great time, and then I'll see a dad give a mom an extra-long hug, and I'll feel that thing you feel on the inside. That sinking feeling. Or we'll get out of the car at a ball game and walk over to the bleachers as a family, and I'm so proud to be with my kids. But then I feel that "thing" again as soon as I see the other families coming—with dads.

Sometimes I am lonely because I am physically alone, like when the kids are with their dad or I'm in another empty hotel room that looks exactly like the last empty hotel room. But sometimes it's lonely because there is no one to share my grown-up heart with. No one to dream with about remodeling the kitchen. No one to hold me after I've tucked in all the kids. No one to whisper, "I'm here," when there is a noise in the night.

I'm guessing you have your own hundred versions of lonely too. So, hey there, lonely girl, what are we going to do about it? How are we going to live with a loneliness woven through every day and still run after an amazing life? Here are some of my ideas. I am deciding that I have to admit to the truth of lonely, but I do not have to live in bondage to it.

lonely integrity

After suffering through some serious bouts of loneliness, I have come to appreciate why a normally rational, intelligent, moral woman would do something stupid. I think I really get it. I now understand why women *think* they've become desperate enough to do incredibly dumb things. They get on planes to meet strange men they just "met" in a chat room. They begin drinking in the dark to mask the pain. Decide to give gambling a try. Buy things they can't afford. Watch things they wouldn't have been caught dead seeing before, and an entire assortment of other immoral, illicit, embarrassing behaviors. They become women they are not, just to feel something other than pain. These women are choosing from their emptiness. And when you are desperately empty and alone, you'll do almost anything to make that feeling go away.

Here is where you and I must be honest with ourselves. The truth is, *we* could become these women. None of us is above choosing out of loneliness. I could *easily* become a foolish woman if I didn't pay attention. I am absolutely determined that I will not succumb to empty choosing, but I'd be crazy not to realize it could happen to me. You and I might become desperately lonely, and it may be some of the most excruciating emotional pain we have ever experienced; but above all else and no matter what happens or doesn't ever happen, we must decide to live with integrity. We must choose integrity so that we can live honorably, and we must choose integrity for our children.

I realize exactly what I am asking you to do. I am a forty-three-year-old single woman trying to live with integrity every day. Most of the time it's a no-brainer. We are grown-ups. Mature and intelligent. Most of us don't purposely make poor choices. Besides, we've seen enough of the consequences of choosing poorly by now, and no one really wants more consequences. But sometimes choosing integrity means that the loneliness is magnified.

I know this is going to sound crazy, but I am a married-man magnet. Me, a single mother of four. It's shocking, I know, but it's true—at least, true enough to be funny. About the only place I meet men is on an airplane, and I don't think I have ever met an unmarried, old-enough-to-go-on-a-date man on one. Just married men, mostly on their way to meetings. And the ridiculous part is, a lot of those married men send me e-mails through my Web site. They are mostly just "nice to meet you" e-mails. My assistant gets them before I do. She laughs at me, the married-man magnet, lets me read them too, and then deletes them. I never respond. Never. But if I ever *was* tempted to respond, I bet it would be when I'm lonely.

When I am tired, I am prone to feeling lonely.

When I am overwhelmed or stressed, I fall easily into loneliness.

When I am disappointed or rejected, I can become sad—and lonely.

I am just a woman who could fall, like anyone else, but I must step up onto higher ground, be aware of my weakness, and do whatever it takes to live right.

When do you feel the loneliest? Several years ago, I realized that I make it through the day fairly well. I'm a morning person. All my best energy pops me out of bed and gets me going strong. Lonely may pang every once in a while, but during the day it can't really get a hold on me. I'm busy, productive, loving my kids, running our home, and mostly staying out of emotional trouble. But nighttime is a different story. If I was going to be sad or troubled, it would be sure to happen after I got the children into bed. Old Lonely would set in and, coupled with fatigue, make me feel desperately empty and alone.

I began to talk to other women, and for many of them,

their most difficult time of day was also at night, between 9 and 11 p.m. Turns out that whenever they'd made a poor choice or acted out of emptiness, it was at the end of the day, when their energy was low and their willpower was sapped. I knew I wasn't any different from these honest women, so I had to do *something* to avoid the same choices.

I decided to start going to bed early. I wanted to believe that I would never give in to "emptiness temptation," but I didn't want to set myself up to fail either. So I decided just to cut out those hours from my day.

My neighbors think I'm crazy. But they also know not to call after nine at night. Within minutes of then, I have taken a Tylenol PM, put the kids to bed, scratched their backs, loved on each one, and fallen peacefully asleep. It's amazing what going to bed early did for this lonely girl. Lonely is still present sometimes, but it doesn't taunt me late at night. It doesn't play with my weakness. It doesn't tempt me to choose poorly. Maybe one day I'll have a reason to stay up, but for now my best "lonely" avoidance is just going to bed.

Lisa called the other night when the kids were away. "What are you doing?" she asked.

"Just over here alone with my dang integrity," I told her.

"Oh, stop it," she said, laughing. "Take your integrity and go to bed."

What do you need to do to avoid the temptation that comes to you during loneliness? Go to bed early? Never travel alone? Give someone else continuous access to your computer history? Cut up your credit cards? Spend the night at a girlfriend's house while your kids are away?

The answer will be different for each of us, but whatever it is for you, I am asking you to not make *any* decision based on your loneliness. Don't pursue a relationship just because you are lonely. Don't give in to your emptiness and start rationalizing dishonest or immoral behavior. And don't get in your car and drive to places you shouldn't be just because it's lonely at home with all that integrity. Set your mind above reproach, and determine to do whatever it takes to live with strength.

Let's hear it for single moms without secret sin and stupid consequences. Who needs one more thing to worry about? We have plenty as it is.

lessons from a lonely mom

LONELY CAN'T KILL YOU. I know it feels like you might die, but we are going to live through this. Sure, lonely multiplies the tears. Lonely can even steal your hope and make you *think* nothing good is coming, but it can't kill you. Half of us would be dead by now if it could.

GOD SEES YOU. A couple of years ago, a church in Mississippi wanted me to speak at their women's conference on Valentine's Day weekend. I agreed to. Then my management team called a few days later. "Angela," they said, "are you sure you want to be out of town that weekend? It's Valentine's Day. Don't you want to stay home?"

I told them, "My kids will be with their dad. What else do I have to do? Let's go."

That weekend eventually rolled around, and I flew to

Mississippi to speak on Friday night and then Saturday morning, Valentine's Day. It was a great conference, and the women had outdone themselves with the theme. There were roses and hearts and chocolates everywhere. Friday night rocked, and I was excited about Saturday morning. The whole idea was for the ladies to have the morning out, then go home to the ones they love, reserving Saturday night for special, romantic dinners and ballroom dancing and all the things people do when they're in love.

On Saturday morning, I awoke early to style my hair for the ladies, put on my best wool suit with really cute boots, and pack my luggage for my afternoon flight. Never mind that an awful storm had arrived in the middle of the night. By the time I pulled my bags and myself outside to my awaiting ride, I was a total disaster. All that work on my hair, and it was stuck to my head. And wet wool smells bad.

I remember thinking, *This was not how I wanted to start this day.*

We arrived at the church, and it was Valentine's Day, so the whole morning had an extra measure of energy. It was one of the coolest things ever to talk to those women about the love of God on the very day everyone wants most to be loved. I told them God calls them beautiful, and it's time to live as though it's true.

But in spite of my laughter and enthusiasm, there was an emptiness inside—just this little thing that would jab me every so often. You see, no one had tucked sweet little notes into my luggage. No flowers had been delivered to my room. No candy hearts. No box of chocolates. I checked my phone at the breaks. No calls. No text messages. *At least one of those kids could call and tell me they love their mama*, I thought. Nothing. And that little thing would jab me in the side again, reminding me I was alone.

At the end of the conference, I hugged all the women and jumped in the car for the drive back to the Jackson airport. The storm was unrelenting, so we drove in wind and rain all the way there. I was taking a commuter to Atlanta to get to another city that night for another meeting in another hotel. Normally there is a covered Jetway out to the plane, but not that afternoon. The attendant gave every flier a Mary Poppins umbrella for the walk to the jet, but it didn't matter. The wind and rain were blowing sideways, and I was soaked by the time I stumbled into my seat. When you're sitting on a jet, on Saturday night, Valentine's Day, soaking wet, in a stinking wool suit, lonely quickly becomes grumpy.

Finally I arrived in Atlanta a couple of hours late, and as I pulled my bag behind me, down the concourse to the next flight, I prayed, *God, just get me to tomorrow, because tomorrow won't be Valentine's Day, and I'll be able to breathe again.* We had just had a wonderful day at the conference, but I was tired and wilted and lonely as heck. I moped toward my gate, feeling as unloved and unnoticed as a woman could feel.

Then, out of the corner of my eye, I spied one of the most handsome men I have ever seen. He must have been mid-seventies, with dark hair and eyes and dressed immaculately. He was very distinguished. So when I saw him over on the left, I pulled my bag as far to the right as I could go. I didn't want him to smell my wet wool suit.

But then I felt a touch on my sleeve. I turned to see who it was, and there was that handsome man.

"Yes?" I mumbled, looking right into those dark, romantic eyes.

"You are vaaary beau-tee-ful," he said in a thick Italian accent.

I was stunned but heard myself say, "Thank you," as he turned to walk away.

My eyes instantly filled with tears, because I knew what had just happened. If that man had said anything else to me, it wouldn't have meant what it meant that day. I knew God Himself had just walked across Concourse B. He had spoken to me the very words I had said to the other women all weekend. *You're beautiful.*

I almost began weeping aloud, doubled over from the sweetness of it all. *Thank You, O God! You see me. You really, really see me. Thank You for coming tonight, on Valentine's Day, to tell me that I am beautiful to You. And the accent . . . that was the bomb.*

I don't know how God is going to come to you. I don't know if someone will walk across the dairy aisle or send an e-mail or leave flowers by your door. Maybe God will speak to you through the Bible or deep into your spirit through prayer. I just know that He sees you and He sees me. Your heartache does not go unnoticed. He holds us through our loneliness. And that night, knowing God sees me was enough.

LONELY IS BETTER THAN LONELY AND IN A MISERABLE RELATIONSHIP. OK, tonight is another Saturday night, and I'm at home alone. It's 7:30 p.m., and I'm in the family room, watching the NCAA World Series. The Tar Heels are winning, but there is no one here to cheer with me. Or sing the fight song. Or wear their Carolina T-shirts. It's kind of lonely sitting in this room by myself. Tar Heel games should be shared. Someone should be yelling beside me.

But you know what? No one has said one mean thing to me all day. No arguments. No conflict. No one is mad at me. When the game is over, I'll go to bed in peace and get up happy and go to church. I have no complaints today. I'm just a little lonely.

But I'll take this version of lonely every time. This kind of lonely makes you wish the phone would ring. But lonely *and* miserable makes you want to jump off of a bridge. So we can do this. Just a little lonely is a million times better than lonely *plus* more pain.

LONELY CAN TEACH YOU HOW TO LOVE THE PEOPLE YOU LOVE. My kids are coming home tonight from a two-week vacation. I have missed them like crazy, and it's all I can do to sit still and wait for them to pull into the driveway. Once I heard a woman say, "I sleep better when the house is full." That's me. I'm just better when they are here. With their friends. And the back door is slamming, and boys are yelling, and food is flying. It makes me happy. This extremely quiet, retirement-home silence makes me lonely.

But the people I love are coming home. So I am clearing my schedule. The next days are all about them. Looking at them. Hearing their stories. Making their favorite pumpkin chip muffins. Loading up the garage refrigerator with Powerade and Popsicles. Even the idea of washing their grimy clothes makes me glad. I have cleared out the laundry room, so I'm ready. Anxious to love the people I love. Excited to show them how special they are and how missed they have been.

Lonely has an upside. It can teach you to love if you'll let it.

• • •

I realize that acquiring lessons from lonely is a little like getting an A in trigonometry. The class was hard, the homework took forever, and now you have mastered a semester of formulas that, quite possibly, you could have lived a lifetime without. There are probably only twenty people in the world who need to know trig. The rest of us might never recite the Pythagorean theorem again as long as we live and do just fine. But there you are, with an A in cosines and tangents, learning things that make you a multilayered person. Interesting. Well versed in the language of science and math.

But lonely is the class nobody wants. Yeah, it gives you layers. Living through it makes us women of great character and internal strength. I tell my friends I did not want this much character. They laugh, but I mean it. I would have been just fine with shallow.

But here we are, single moms with kids, somehow forced into the advanced-placement class on lonely, and certain we could have lived the rest of our lives without all this instruction.

Maybe somewhere down the road the test will be over and we'll place out of lonely.

Graduate-level love *must* be next.

4

tired and guilty mom

A while back I read a line on a page-a-day calendar that said, "Save the best for your family." That torn-off motivation was promptly taped to my bathroom mirror, where it stayed for at least a year. But every day since, the instruction to save the best of me for my kids has tugged at my heart, usually a tug of inspiration quickly followed by another tug of guilt.

I want to. I dream about the days when I am giving the best of me to them, and in my dream I have taken the whole family to the lake on a perfect summer afternoon. We swim together and play on the shore, and then (miraculously) I have prepared a delicious home-cooked picnic for all of us, plus twenty friends. I want to be Dreamy Mom, who gets it right and loves with boundless energy and creativity. I want to love them like crazy and be consistent with the demonstration of my love. But I am so afraid that more often than thinking of me as Amazing Mom, the children just think of me as tired.

Last night I went to bed tired. Actually, "tired" is a ridiculous understatement. More like "completely spent." Exhausted. Or as they say in North Carolina, "worn slap out." This past weekend I had a difficult travel night that scared me and flattened me emotionally. A canceled flight. A 2 a.m. cab ride with a lost driver. I never made it to the vouchered hotel. After three hours of sleep and another difficult, delayed return trip, I finally made it back home to my kids the next day.

The moment I walked through the door, Grayson and I began working on his science-fair project, testing the absorbency, wet strength, and value of six different kinds of paper towels. I'll save you the trouble of doing your own controlled and calculated experiments: buy Viva. Last night we were finally putting the presentation board together, I hadn't packed for the next four days away, and my printer ink ran out right in the middle of the hypothesis statement. You get the picture. I was totally at the end of myself. I don't scream anymore when I'm empty; I just walk around like a zombie, on the verge of tears, fighting back the urge to give up and run away.

All night, the kids kept looking at me with sad eyes, coming over to hug me every so often. They knew I had hit the wall, so they tippy-toed lightly around my heart. Grayson probably told me ten times, "I love you, Mom." What a sweetheart. I love them too. Hate science-fair projects with a purple passion, but I love those kids "like a fat kid loves cake," as my daughter would say.

About seven o'clock, my friend Lisa was at the house, helping pull together my travel. Grayson and I were looking for more pennies to add to the wet-strength test. Who knew that a wet paper towel clamped over the sides of a bowl could hold about five dollars in pennies? The little kids kept walking through the study with bags of chips, asking what we were having for dinner. I looked at Lisa across the chaos and said, as truthfully as I have ever spoken, "I don't think I can do this. I'm not going to make it this time." I was serious, and she knew it.

"Just do the next thing," she said.

"I can't."

"Angela, yes, you can," she said, firmly but lovingly.

So I went into the kitchen and made quesadillas.

And I drove to the store to buy ink.

And I came home to print out science-experiment data.

And I laid out four days of grown-up, speaker-girl clothes.

And I ironed the wrinkled white shirt that goes with everything.

And I scratched every back and prayed every prayer and tucked in the people I love most in the world.

And I brushed my teeth.

And I did *not* wash my face or put on wrinkle cream but went straight to bed, feeling guilty—a little guilty about my dirty face with no wrinkle cream, but mostly guilty because I want to give my kids the best of me. Sometimes they seem to only get what's left. And too many days there is nothing.

• • •

I recently cried through these words from *To Own a Dragon*, a heartrending book about growing up fatherless. Author Donald Miller writes about his mom:

> She mothered herself into exhaustion. Weekdays, Mom would work late, often coming home right around our bedtime, and even then we were all too tired to act like a family. I knew, somehow, that my mother's long working hours were because of my sister and me. But I never thought to ascribe my mother's emotional and physical exhaustion to the lack of a husband and father, rather, I ascribed it to my existence. There were times, I confess, I wondered if my family would be better off without me. I grew up believing that if I had never been born, things would be easier for the people I loved. (Donald Miller and John MacMurray [NavPress, 2006], 47)

This passage hit a little too close to home. I am so very tired. The end of me usually arrives a couple of hours before the end of the day. I trudge down the hall to tuck everyone in, given out, sad even, that another day has come and gone and I am not more energetic. Sometimes the kids tell me, "Mom, you look tired." I smile and mumble, "I am, honey." And now I wonder if they believe it's their fault.

The truth is, the things I gripe at my kids about could all become miraculously perfected and I'd *still* be tired. Each child could get his or her grimy clothes to the laundry room, never again whack brother or sister with a rolled-up bath towel, rinse the dirty cereal bowl before kindly putting it in the dishwasher, do the homework without being reminded, and push the trash-can to the end of the driveway on Thursday nights. They could all be perfect kids and I'd still be exhausted. Happy, but pooped. It's just the single-mom dilemma. We are everything to everybody for a very, very long time. It makes a lot of sense for one woman who is running the world to feel like this.

As I finished reading Donald and John's book, several things stuck with me, but addressing my own personal exhaustion and how it impacts my mothering is the one I wanted to deal with first. So I began at the only place I ever know where to begin. I began to pray about being tired.

Not that I can't keep up the pace, because I can. I've already proven that to myself, to God, and to everyone who knows me. I can do this whole thing tired if I have to. But I believe that this level of sustained exhaustion could leave the children with more than a taste of Donald's pain. My exhaustion could begin to feel like salt rubbed in the open wounds they already suffer. I don't want that. More than I can say, I don't want to hurt them anymore. It's already been hard enough.

my tired lessons

SOMETHING HAS TO CHANGE. This is one chapter in which I am completely writing each word in process. I am not looking back at lessons I have attained, but forward to what still needs to happen in my own life. Really and truly, some-thing has to change. I cannot continue to live at breakneck speed. I know it's becoming increasingly unhealthy for me and for the children.

When I became a single mom, I shot myself out of a cannon trying to prove that I could both take care of us *and* work just as hard as anyone being our sole provider. I never said no to anything, and even as I have become busier, I have taken almost every opportunity that has come to me. Each year, I have feared that the kind of work I do would just dry up and go away. I have neither an employment contract nor a paycheck on the first and the fifteenth. No corporate retirement, health benefits, or paid vacations. Just me. I have been insecure, and my insecurity has often fueled my decisions. My decisions have left me without margins. And no margins means no time for adequate rest and renewal, even with that nine o'clock bedtime.

I imagine that you and I are in the same place. I don't know one single mom who gets enough rest or renewal. We live like wild women, part of us just proving that we can, the other part desperate and without options.

The other day a guy said, "I have nothing left to prove." *Yeah, me too*, I thought, then realized that the truth is, I have a lot left to prove. I have to get four kids raised. And then get them through college. Even without graduate school, that's another fifteen years in front of me. And I have to keep feeding these blessings and clothing them and loving them. I know I can't keep going like this, sprinting from one need to the next. I am living in the ridiculous.

I believe God is asking two things of me. Faith and pacing.

A NEW FAITH FOR A NEW SEASON. In almost every area of my life, I have staked all my decisions and beliefs on the truth of God's existence. I am unwaveringly convinced of His abiding love for me and the children, His faithfulness to care for us and protect us. I believe in God with all my life, but in this area of racing from thing to thing, I have been living as if I doubt.

As I have begun to pray, I realize I have trusted God in many ways for many things, but now it's time to trust Him enough to say to others, "No" and "Not now." This is new for me. In the beginning, I saw every job opportunity as God's amazing provision for me. Each time the phone rang with work, I blessed God for giving me a way to provide. I am still so very grateful, but God requires me to engage my faith and choose wisely with my time. I am only one woman with only these four children. I cannot miss their growing up because I am afraid to say no to every opportunity that comes.

A few days ago I returned from a two-week trip to South Africa. The conferences where I spoke were amazing, and I was absolutely sure I had been appointed for that time and that work. But I also decided that I couldn't go again without my children. To leave them crying in the driveway and me crying all the way to the airport was one of the worst mom moments of my life. I promised God, "I will not go this far or be away this long again without them. If You want me to travel like this, You will have to provide for all of us."

During the second conference, some women approached me about coming to do a citywide event in Cape Town sometime next year. I told them I'd love to, but I'd made a commitment not to travel that far again without my children. I'd have to bring all of them if I came. Without hesitation they replied, "Oh, that wouldn't be a problem at all. The finances are available. We'd be delighted to bring your whole family. We'll entertain the kids at the beach and organize a safari after you're done." I stood there smiling at God. New faith meant stepping out and trusting Him to care about us being together.

I talk about God all the time, but He never ceases to teach me more and more about the depths of His love and the next place of faith I need to grow into.

PACING FOR A MARATHON. I am wired with a lot of energy, and it drives my assistant crazy. In the office, I will think I'm multitasking, talking a mile a minute about each item that we have to address, giving instructions, making decisions—all in all, sprinting through the day's work so that I can get that part done and move on to the next thing. But Lisa doesn't call it multitasking; she jokingly calls it ADD. I can't tell you how many times she's said, "Stop it with the ADD and go back to the third thing you said."

I do not have ADD, but I do move fast and think fast. And as much as I whine about it sometimes, I obviously like my life that way. As the firstborn child, I remember always being afraid I was going to miss something. I think I'm still afraid to miss anything, so I just keep finagling ways to make everything happen. You probably already realize what happens with that kind of planning: I hang myself all the time. Too much. Counting on the schedule to run seamlessly. Pushing myself too far. And trying to sprint back-to-back races that I have made up for myself to run.

I am sure God is speaking to me about pacing myself and my family. Rather than marathon living—and especially marathon mothering—building in more time to linger in conversation, shoot baskets, or watch an episode of *Gilmore Girls* with Taylor. Pacing for emotional and spiritual energy even when my body thinks I can keep going.

My calendar is booked close to two years in advance. I can tell you today when I have time off next year and what night I'm available to have dinner next spring. In the past I would see an open space on my calendar and fill it. Most of the time I schedule good things, like a vacation or a weekend with a girlfriend. Now my personal marathon commitment is to leave the open space alone. Less busyness and more pacing. Leaving margins.

SOMETIMES YOU NEED A BOUNDARY. SOMETIMES YOU CAN JUST KEEP PUSHING. Two years ago, at the end of my South African conference weekend, my host, Cathy, pulled me aside.

"Angela, there is something I want to talk to you about. There is a book I think you should get and a workbook I want you to do. I am concerned and believe you must do this soon. The book is called *Boundaries*. Have you heard of it?"

Of course I knew of the ultra-best-selling books on boundaries. I even have a few on my bookshelf, but I wasn't sure why Cathy was so insistent I read this one.

"I think you are pushing too hard," she said, "and I'm afraid you are going to burn out if you don't learn to say no to people. You can't sign books for hours. You can't speak to everyone who wants to talk to you. You need boundaries to protect yourself. I want you to finish well, not crash and burn."

I really took her tender instruction to heart as I packed my things and headed back to the States that weekend. I kept asking myself what boundaries looked like for me. I like people. I like hearing their stories. I like kids in my house. I like a little crazy with my orderly life. I decided to keep pondering her wisdom and ask God for clear direction.

Two weeks later, at a meeting of Christian booksellers, as God would have it, I was introduced to the authors of *Boundaries*, Drs. Henry Cloud and John Townsend. As soon as it was semi-polite, I stepped across every professional restraint and sought John's advice. I told him about Cathy's concern for my boundaries and asked for his opinion.

Without knowing all the details, he said, "Sometimes you need a boundary. When saying yes will cause you harm or contribute to an unhealthy lifestyle, then boundaries are essential. But you don't make boundaries just for the sake of making boundaries. If you like meeting the women and it doesn't hurt you to keep going, then do that. Have fun, but learn to recognize when you are stepping across the line and when it's time to say, 'I'd love to, but I can't.'"

John really set me free that day, free to say no when saying yes would push me beyond mental or physical health. And free to say yes as long as it's not harmful to me or the ones I love. I am learning to stop before my schedule gets absurd, even though I enjoy hard work and long days of people, and sometimes that is a healthy tired.

WHEN YOU WORK HARD, YOU GET TIRED. Being tired is not the worst thing to happen to any of us. My friend Louise says, "This is what you are supposed to feel like when you

my single mom life

work hard." Managing a life and a home is not a day at the spa. Your muscles hurt. Headaches happen. Physical and emotional energy runs out, and we need to be refilled. Much of that is OK. It's our humanity. To work is good, and good work makes you tired.

It's the unhealthy, excessive, driven exhaustion that's getting to us. It's the always-tired mom that my kids see that worries me. I don't want them to look back and only remember that Mom was exhausted. It's OK to get tired, but it's also OK to be rested, with a little free time and nothing in particular to do.

my guilty lessons

Amazing how most of us quickly follow up our tiredness with guilt. I wanted my kids to grow up in "the happy house," but I'm sure it feels more as if they are growing up in "the tired house," with a mom who mostly says, "Not now, baby. Maybe we can do that later." Of course, I don't just feel guilty about being too tired to play. I have an entire unwritten list of guilt reminders. But you know what? You don't have to be a single mom to struggle with guilt. It's the worldwide mom condition. Read these words I wrote about ten years ago, when I was a married mom.

> The greatest burden to come from the supermom fantasy is the sometimes lifelong battle with guilt. I wrestle with the ever-present feeling that I could and should be doing everything better. I should make cookies more often. I should read to every child every night. I should make scrapbooks. I

should be in their classrooms more and be available to go on all the field trips. I should pray more, sleep less, look better, exercise, and all in all, just be more fun. For as many areas as there are in my life, there are opportunities to feel guilty.

Guilt is a great weapon in the hands of Satan. He uses it to rob mothers of their joy and move them into more "doing" instead of "being." I feel the attacks and it tears the life out of me. As I look into the kitchen right now, I see two piles of laundry on the table. I could feel guilty for spending these quiet moments writing and get up and fold clothes. But then "doing" wins; instead, I am choosing my passion. (Angela Thomas, *Tender Mercy for a Mother's Soul* [Tyndale, 2001], 15)

Just being a mom means there is guilt to battle, maybe a different version now that we're single, but it comes with being the mom either way.

THERE IS A WRONG GUILT. The wrong kind of guilt moves you and me into "doing." We host bigger birthday parties and give better presents, mostly fueled by divorce/solo-parent guilt, for me. And then there are the various seasons of striving, where I subconsciously try to prove that I can do it or build it or dream it, or whatever. When I meet a woman who is striving, there is usually a countenance about her that is fairly repulsive. I look back and cringe when I remember being a "striving" woman. Most of the time it was the product of my solo-parent guilt. You know what I'm talking about. It's the stuff we do so our kids won't have to do without just because they have a single mom. They already have to walk up our driveway to a house with no dad while most of their friends are running home to a really great man. So we convince ourselves that they should have the coolest skateboard shoes the Internet can provide, shipped overnight so their single-parented feet won't have to wait one more day. It's a bunch of hooey, but we've all done it, just before we catch ourselves and feel guilty for overindulging.

The wrong guilt is unhealthy. It will eat your lunch and take away your appetite for dinner. It makes you frantic and unsettled inside. It keeps you ever searching for something better, when, as my grandmother used to say, "the best place on earth is already in your own backyard."

Are you doing more? Caught up in unnecessary activity or striving? Do you feel anxious, sure that you need to do even *more* to compensate for what you will never be able to give? If so, then you probably already know that you are living in a downward spiral. This kind of guilt takes you down and keeps you there.

THERE IS A RIGHT GUILT. The right kind of guilt inspires us to become consistent, secure moms. I wrestle with divorce guilt and how it will affect my kids all the time. What I have asked God to do with my discontent is make me the best possible woman, the best version of me, as a gift to my children. If they're going to have a single mom, I want them to be proud that it's me. I want to live with integrity and act with responsibility so they can count on at least one person in this world to be like that. A person you put your full weight into. A woman who nourishes instead of needs. A woman who is exactly like my dad.

Ever since I can remember, I have been proud to be Joe Thomas's daughter. As a matter of fact, when I was a total nerd without one accomplishment or dream, my best thing was being my daddy's daughter. I loved being wherever he was because he was fun and energetic. You're probably not surprised to hear that he's a storyteller, and I loved it when he told funny stories. It didn't matter where I went in town; when a person found out that I was the daughter of Joe Thomas, his or her gaze always changed. That person looked at me as if I had value. I was the daughter of a very good man. And that very good man lived a life that gave me the deepest security I have ever known. He still does.

If my dad says he will be here at 5 a.m. to pick me up for the airport, I am absolutely sure that he will be here at 4:50, with a cup of coffee, waiting patiently until I come downstairs and raise the garage door. He'll also be smiling, because as far as I can determine, he is always happy. And we will talk about today and the future with optimism and hope and great faith in God. According to my dad, I can do anything. I never had sense enough to not believe him.

Maybe divorce has been good for me. Maybe the good guilt built a fire underneath my "wanna be like that one day" and forced me to start becoming that kind of woman now. What if my children were proud just because I'm their mom? What if it gave them untold security because I have worked on becoming the best version of me? What if being a good woman matters more than anything, and it's the most excellent gift to our kids?

If guilt can do that, then I think it's the best use of a condition that we will all have to live with anyway.

•••

I am a tired and guilty mom. But what's new? Being tired and hearing guilt zing through my head came with the diaper bag. We've all been waging this private battle ever since someone said, "Congratulations! You're a mom." In fact, every mom who ever stirred up a batch of Rice Krispies Treats probably feels tired and guilty. Who knew it would be so tough or last so long? None of us could have known that the single-mom life would biggie-size every hard thing about mothering. We might all agree that it was probably better *not* to have known then what was coming. And maybe the best thing we can do now is just to accept it.

Amy Carmichael is remembered for many wonderful teachings, but among them are the words "In acceptance, there lieth peace." What brilliant, beautiful words of rest. Amy, once known as "the Rescuer of India's Children," mothered thousands of orphaned children during her years as a missionary. It makes sense to me that such profound words were born in the heart of a woman who was mom to so many. I am learning to accept what is, add to that everything I can do, and then accept what has become: accept the *good* tired that comes from good work. Learn to rein in the *exhausted* tired that comes from sprinting without pacing and lack of faith in the One who holds me. Accept that hard work came attached to the dreams of what we always hoped would be. Accept my kids and all the ways they are surprisingly different from what I expected.

I still worry that my children will only remember me dragging at the end of the day, eyes glazed over, and just nodding politely during their late-night stories. But what can I do? Stop taking care of them? Can't happen.

So they'll probably remember that I was tired sometimes. But they'll be OK. And someday, when I'm in the old folks' home, maybe they'll remember how hard I worked to care for them and feel guilty enough to come visit their spunky old mom. And just maybe they'll feed me extra Girl Scout Thin Mint ice cream when all I can do is smile and ask who they are.

At the end of every day, I ask myself, *Given the circumstances and the resources and my energy, have I done all I can?* If the honest answer is yes, then I have learned to accept how things turned out.

Right after I accept what I can't do anything about, I roll my tired body over and go to sleep—and forget about the guilt.

In acceptance, tired and guilty single moms sleepeth in peace.

5

solo-parent mom

I know many single moms who have dreamy coparent-ing relationships with their children's dads. And I'm sure I almost gawk as I watch them interact at school or on the ball field. Those kinds of parents talk side by side at events, communicating calmly concerning decisions for the children. They support one other and adjust their schedules to cover emergencies. They attend parties together. Eat occasional meals together. Unite over discipline and rewards. They act like grown-ups and do whatever it takes to keep the children from feeling ridiculously torn between Mom and Dad.

I have no idea what that's like. I wish I could write a coparenting chapter, but I can't. I'm disqualified. (I *can* refer you to a Web site about coparenting. My friend Tammy Bennett is doing a great job teaching divorced parents how to parent their children together. The Web address is www.christiancoparenting.com.) Here we are, all these years down the road, and my stomach still hurts with every interaction. "Difficult" doesn't even come close to describing it. So I will write to you about solo-parenting. But as I said earlier, I am absolutely sure this is not how it is supposed to be. The whole thing stinks to high heaven. Adults should act like grown-ups. Kids should not have to feel divided and worn out by the underlying drama that goes on between their parents.

If Dad is on the planet, moms shouldn't have to shoulder all the responsibilities, decisions, and futures of our children. But for many of us, even those who have good relationships with their ex-husbands, solo-parenting is a big part of our journey. So, we can whine or we can become amazing moms, solo-parenting our kids the very best way we know how. I knew right from the start that I would do anything to give my kids the best life possible given our particular circumstances. I just didn't know at the beginning how hard it can be to parent alone. Or how lonely and lost it feels not to have someone to talk to or lean on.

When my married-friend moms get tired of reasoning with a child, they can say, when "Dad" comes home, "You take it; I'm done." But when you solo-parent, there is no one coming home to take over. There is no one to bounce your ideas off of, no one to cover your back or reinforce the decisions you've made. No one just to hold you through the tough choices and whisper, "I know you're worn out. I'll handle this."

It's just me. And I'm pretty sure by now that no one is coming home to save me. Like it or not, I'm it. And I am determined to give solo-parenting everything this one woman can give.

solo-realities

I realize that sounds really big, my saying I'm determined to give everything one woman can give. I'm making huge promises to myself and to my kids. You have to know that in my heart, I mean it. I am going to do whatever it takes to parent them well. In my mind, I am resolute. But the realities of parenting solo are truths that have to be reckoned with.

All day long, I am just a human body. I get tired, really, really tired, just like you. Sometimes I can barely hold my eyes open through dinner, much less last through a two-hour *American Idol* that runs till 10. "Mom, please watch this with us," they beg. Other days, I want to cook and *plan* to cook, but the phone rings and the e-mails pile up, and before I know it, the kids are standing in the pantry, looking for a miracle dinner. It's 7 p.m., and I tell them to put their shoes on. El Mexcal will have to do again. Chips and fajitas instead of meat loaf. I always mean to come through, but many times I don't.

And then there is the emotional toll that disciplining children takes on the heart. I get tired of being the bad guy, handing out punishment. Or being gracious and merciful when I just want to spank their bottoms. Creatively correcting their character, redirecting their inclinations, and choosing to be patient when I'm empty and would rather scream.

So I've decided to just do the very best I can in my one-woman, only-two-hands body, and then receive the mercy God has promised when my weakness kicks in.

When parenting four children, there is always more that could have or should have been done. I could have held

AnnaGrace longer after she had a bad dream. I should have made it to William's dairy-farm field trip. I coulda/shoulda done many things differently or better or wholeheartedly. But I can't do it all or do it right every single time. No one can.

So what if we just decide to make the best informed solo decisions that we can? Be available. Show up, wait up, and drive up, every time we are able. Desire to be a great mom every time we are able. Give everything God intended for us to give. And then, what if we rest in the reality of our humanity?

As single parents, we will probably doubt ourselves and our abilities every day until our children are grown. Then we'll cry our old-lady eyes out when, as adults, our kids need years of therapy to help them process all the ways we fell short.

But we must try anyway. These are the years that matter. These are the days of grace or of heartache. If we rally for anything, let us pull ourselves together for this purpose. We can solo-parent if we have to. And we can be really good at it, nowhere near perfect, but good enough to grow these pumpkins up strong.

And those kids, those silly, doe-eyed kids, they belong to God, the God who is not one bit surprised that we parent them alone. They will be OK, because they are His and we've fallen on our knees and entrusted them to the faithful care of their Father. The One who is called Perfect Love will be their covering and their guide.

Every night I close my eyes and speak my need:

O God, they are Yours. Please cover my imperfect parenting with Your mercy. Break heaven loose over their lives. Send

angels to guide where I have misdirected. Guard their bod-
ies and their minds. Cover them with the blood of Jesus, and
set them apart as Yours.

I remember when people used to ask me, "But what about the children?" All I knew to say then and all I still know now is that my children belong to God. They were His before they came to me. Your children belong to God too.

Maybe you've never asked God to cover your imperfect parenting with mercy. But He can and He will as we pray. You can do it too. Maybe today is a great day to begin.

my solo-parenting lessons

DO THE VERY BEST YOU CAN WITH THEIR DAD. For the sake of the children, figure out the best, most sane modes of interaction with your kids' dad. This man is the father of your children. They want to love him, and it's your responsibility to encourage and facilitate a healthy love. Don't hinder or harm their relationship.

If your kids come home from a visitation weekend and tell you things that make you want to bite your tongue off, you don't have to keep silent in fear of saying something that might be perceived as negative. A very wise counselor once said, "You have to address wrong behaviors or attitudes and call them wrong. You do not have to berate or demean, but you are responsible to correct a misleading impression the children may be forming." Handle it just as you would if your kids came home from a sleepover with a friend and told you that the friend didn't tell the truth or made a promise and broke it. "Well, how did that make you feel to be treated like that?" you might say. "Do you understand that truth is important, and when you give your word, you should keep it? I don't want you to imitate your friend, because these character things matter. You see how it hurts other people when you don't have good character. Be strong in what I am teaching you. Even if you see it done differently around you, you and I have to treat people right."

But let's face it: moms and dads are different. Dads may allow certain actions or activities that a mom never would. Sometimes just the opposite is true. So for many single moms, the relationship with their kids' dad is a very tender balance between honoring the man who is the father of their children and dealing with issues that influence character. You will blow it sometimes, and sometimes you'll get it right, but just remember that there are times when someone has to be the grown-up, and it will have to be you. It may help to mentally remove yourself from the situation, even envision yourself standing over the situation, consciously choosing to bring wisdom and common sense, just as an adult mom should be doing for her children.

It may seem as though every week there is something new to navigate or figure out, and you'll need to be able to disconnect enough not to take it personally. This is your life, and you want to stay as sane as possible. I am a big fan of e-mail and text-messaging, because no tone is involved in the communication. Be conflict-avoidant at every opportunity, because it requires too much energy and emotion to enter into the same dead-end discussions yet again. You have kids who need all of the energy you can give, so save it for them.

I am ashamed to admit that it took me years to begin praying for my kids' dad. I do pray for him now. I had prayed before, but not real, pray-like-you-mean-it prayers. It would bless my children for their dad to live in strength, achieving his dreams and accomplishing great things. I have begun to pray with freedom for his blessing. I want my kids to have the best dad ever. They deserve no less. It's finally easy to pray that for them.

FORGET ABOUT WHAT'S FAIR; IT'S ABOUT THE KIDS NOW. I take the kids shopping for their dad for Christmas, his birthday, and Father's Day. They would hate not to have a special gift for him, so I do it for them. Besides, I want them to learn how to be givers. The same gift approach is not reciprocated. So before my birthday or Christmas, I'll call my parents and ask them to take my kids shopping for a gift for me. I don't need one more thing, but this is for the children. They want to give. Kind of unfair, I guess. But it doesn't matter. As we fumble our way through these years and these interactions, I am learning to ask myself, "How will this affect the kids?" Many things that feel unfair to me may in reality be ridiculously unfair. But if it's not about me and just about the children, I have learned to let it go, do what's right for them, and interact with their dad as best I can. Deciding that this relationship is not about me anymore has brought tremendous freedom. I can do what the kids need. Hallelujah! It's just about the children now.

I AM THE MOM; I AM IN CHARGE. Maybe we feel to blame for our circumstances. Maybe we doubt our abilities. But each of us is still "the mom." We're in charge. We are grown-up, and they are little, even if their "little" is packaged inside tall teenage bodies. The authority for parenting has been given to us by God. Single-mom status doesn't take away that authority or diminish our responsibility to God to protect, guide, discipline, and lead.

My kids' eyes glaze over like a Krispy Kreme doughnut when I say it, but I usually fall back on this one at least once a week: "I am responsible to God for your protection. This really isn't about you or being your friend or what you think in that head of yours. This is about *me*, answering to God for how I have protected *you*. I don't care if it makes you mad or sad or glad. I am the mom. I will stand in front of God one day, and I'm taking that seriously."

And you know what? It gives my kids a deep sense of security when I stand up and lead with authority. I can see it in their countenances. When I take charge, I'm not mean or difficult, but I'm searching for wisdom to direct their hearts and maintain healthy boundaries.

Almost every Sunday after church, we grab a quick lunch at a restaurant. And almost every Sunday there is a disagreement about where to go. I could eat Mexican food at every meal. Grayson wants stir-fry. The others chime in about greasy drive-thru. Some time back, I said to them, "My daddy never asked us where we wanted to go after church. We all just got in the car, and he drove to wherever he wanted us to eat. Then we ate lunch without grumbling. And no little kids got to weigh in about where the best kid toys were. We just went in and acted grateful. I think I'm going to be like Papa. I'll drive; you get out and eat when I stop."

Last Sunday, we got in the car after church, and the usual bickering began right on schedule. But then Taylor piped up from the back: "Mom, just be like Papa."

They need us to lead, in the little things like food and in the big things about home and heart. Don't be afraid to be the mom. These children need to be children, and that happens when you and I step into our roles with strength and gracious authority.

SAY NO WHEN YOUR HEART SAYS NO. I believe that when you ask God for direction, He will give it. As a single mom, I feel as if I am talking to God all the time. The harder thing is listening to His answers, discerning His will, and then trusting that God's way is the best way, even if it frustrates the kids or makes a situation more difficult for me. I am learning to say no when I feel that "God thing" on the inside. It's the way I've come to hear from God with regard to parenting the children.

A few years ago, Taylor met some girls who wanted her to come hang out one Saturday. I talked to the mom, got directions, and agreed to take Taylor over.

When I pulled up in the driveway, every Holy Spirit alarm inside me went off. It was as though I could feel a darkness. But for some dumb reason, I still let Taylor go in and stay for the agreed time. When I came back later to pick her up, I had the same sick feeling in my stomach. *I shouldn't have let her go in there.*

When Taylor got in the car, I told her, "Honey, I know you are going to think I am the weirdest person you know, but warning sirens are going off inside of me. I don't know these people. I don't know what they do. I am not accusing anyone of anything, but there is a presence of evil here, and I will not let you come back. The girls can come to our house, but I have decided that you cannot be here."

I think Taylor was in the eighth grade then. Not one of our best years. She just sat there, discouraged, I'm sure, staring out the car window, probably thinking that her mom was a total loon. But the feeling was so strong that day that I stuck by my gut. The next time she was invited over, I said she couldn't go but offered to pick up the girls and bring them to our house. Taylor was mortified.

"Mom, all my friends think you don't like them," my beautiful, goofball teenager accused. I guess she thought I cared what thirteen-year-olds think of me.

"Well, I don't," I told her.

"Moooooom, I can't believe you said that," moaned the sad one.

"Honey, you know I love those girls," I told her. "I do care about their hearts and their lives. I care about the choices they make and the consequences they will suffer. I want you to know they are always welcome here. I will talk with them. I will feed them. I will do anything to care for their tender hearts. But I will not lay my daughter on their altar. *You can't go.*"

That was about the end of the conversation. Weird Mom going on her "Holy Spirit hesitation" keeps eighth-grade daughter from hanging out at a friend's house. I think it was a pretty

my single mom life

awful day for her. I'm sure she made something up to tell them instead of the Holy Spirit part. She probably moped around. I didn't mind. I knew she was safe.

And here's the kicker. About three months later, I ran into a mom at the grocery store who knew these new "friends." "Tell me about the girls," I said to her. It turns out that even though I didn't have any details, my heart had been right. There were more reasons for Taylor to stay away than I could have imagined. I can't tell you how many times God has used that *no* in my heart to help me guide the children. When I feel that thing on the inside, I don't care what they say or how many promises they make; the answer is unequivocally *no*.

When your heart says no, you have to go with it. I always try to explain to my children the whys. And I usually blame God when I do. I'll tell them that I have asked God to direct me, and when I have that sick feeling about something, it's usually Him getting my attention and prompting me to tell them no. They've seen this one prove itself so many times now that, even though they don't like to hear it, they usually rest in the decision.

SAY YES EVERY TIME YOU CAN. One of the things that makes saying no easier for my kids to swallow is their belief that I am working to say yes every time I can. I really do try to say yes as often as I am able. Life goes by too fast, and their sweet little growing-up days will soon be over. So if it's good, if it might be fun, if we can afford it, if they have done their homework and finished their chores, then I try to say yes. Sometimes all that *hasn't* been done, but I say yes anyway.

They are really good kids, and every once in a while it's okay to be indulged with a yes that you didn't quite deserve.

BE THE FIRST TO APOLOGIZE WHEN YOU BLOW IT.

How will they know how to do this unless we model for them the humility of "I'm sorry"? I want my kids to realize when they have chosen or acted poorly and then learn to seek forgiveness and restoration quickly. I am the one who is teaching them, so I have to model this kind of gentleness.

On the other side, when your child says, "I'm sorry," then it's over. There may be consequences, but the offense is over. We can't berate our children for their mistakes or keep reminding them of their bad decision. Your tone and your countenance must communicate that "it's over." Forgiveness really forgives.

I remember hearing that we should treat our family as friends and our friends as family. I believe that is especially true in parenting. We correct, make and accept apologies, and then rebuild in tenderness with our children. Their hearts are so precious, and no kid should have to endure the pain of grudge holding or conditional forgiveness. Teach them how to give and receive forgiveness.

REVERSE YOURSELF WHEN NECESSARY. Many moms

have said to me, "Angela, I have already allowed my kids to do such-and-such, so how can I say no to them now?" One of the best things I have learned about these times is that it is very grown-up to reverse yourself if you realize you have made a mistake or not chosen what is best.

I have often had to say something like this to my kids: "I know I have allowed this in the past, but now I believe I was wrong. I didn't hold a strong boundary for our family. I made a poor choice. But now I know better, so I want to do better for all of us. I realize this may be difficult for you, but I am reversing myself. It would be wrong of me to let something go by when I know it's not best for you or for me. Please forgive me for not doing this sooner or for making you feel confused."

They may grumble or whine, but kids do very well with honesty. I have reversed myself several times after I became better informed or felt that the boundary needed to be tighter in a certain area. The key to parenting in strength is that when you reverse yourself, you have to stay there. No slip-sliding away from your newfound wisdom or direction. The kids will lose respect for your authority. The last thing you want them to think is, *Yeah, she always says stuff like that, but she never means it.*

TALK TO THE CHILDREN AS THOUGH YOU ARE FASCI-NATED BY THEIR LIVES. How would you greet your best friend? Greet your children the same. Go to them every time they come home. Hug them. Look into their eyes with intention and love. Give them at least five minutes to get their bearings, find a snack, and settle in before you begin barking orders or correcting their wrongs.

Track with their conversations. William, who is ten, had me alone for a few minutes yesterday. He wanted to talk to me about drawing Nintendo characters on cards to send to the company. He has already done an entire collection, and he's hoping they'll want to use his drawings for card packs. I cannot tell you how lost I was with every name that came after Mario. And I have no idea what they do. But I had to track with him so he'd know that he is valuable. So valuable, in fact, that he had me on the computer, Googling the Nintendo International address so he can send them his art. I had a million other things to do, but respecting my baby's heart and his interests always trumps a book deadline or a pile of laundry.

One of the gifts my parents gave to me was their interest in my life and its details. My dad waited up for me every night after I began to drive. We always spent fifteen or twenty minutes together, with me telling him who I'd seen that evening and where we went. He asked questions, probably more for my protection, and he always showed me he was interested. He still talks to me that way, as though my life is captivating to him. What a gift we'll give our children when we decide to be fascinated with their details.

DON'T GIVE THEM EVERYTHING. We have a pang of guilt—*The kids live in a broken home*—so we buy something we can't afford or they don't need just to make us all feel that we're not broken. But indulgent spending is not only a waste of money; it's also poor parenting. Obviously, some stuff is OK. But I also think a little boredom is OK. Just yesterday, William ran into the house with his buddies. They wanted me to take them to the store to buy a new video game because they were "bored." It was beautiful outside. They thought they had played every outside thing they could think of, but I was absolutely sure that no one needed a new video game with perfect weather like we had.

I told the boys that if they were truly bored, it might be time to scrub the bathtub; then they could clean out the garage; and after that, the deck needed sweeping. Magically, they were immediately *un*bored. Kids do need help filling up their time and learning to be creative, but we do not have to give them everything they ask for to make that happen.

ASK A MAN LIKE DAVE OR MIKE OR RICK TO BE THE TOUGH GUY SOMETIMES. Dave, Mike, and Rick are all married to beautiful women. They have three kids each. All are great dads who love their families well. And all three of those men live on my street. Those good men also help me parent my kids. Many times I am totally out of my element or just tired of hearing the sound of my voice. And sometimes my kids just need a man. God bless these men; they have plenty to do at their own houses, but they have each stepped in to help me parent my children.

The guys especially help with my sons: Frisbee golf around the neighborhood, coaching their baseball teams, taking them to practice and skate parks and the pool and camping. And lately, I've asked each of these good men to be the tough guy for me. Mom is tired.

Dave reminds my boys when it's time to mow the yard. Funny how they jump right on it when he tells them. Rick sits all the boys down for air-soft safety lessons or tree-house policy or anger management. Mike polices flashlight tag and takes them for burgers. All these men have my permission to treat my children as their own. And it's really making a difference, both for the kids and for me.

Maybe you need to ask someone too. Someone with a heart of love. Someone cool. Someone who can say the same thing you just said, but different enough to be heard.

• • •

Even though I'm blessed to have some great guy neighbors, some days I look around and ask, "Why in the world do I have to do this alone? *Those* women don't have to parent by themselves. *She* has a good man to help. *That* mom has a soft place to fall. Why not me?"

But there are no good answers.

Single moms are solo parents. And it's just tough.

So I don't know why. Many times, I don't know *how*.

Maybe if we just keep doing the best we can, surely God will make one enough.

6

boundary mom

After a few of my babies became toddlers, I began to understand why parents yell across the room at their little ones. Sometimes it's easier to yell than to actually get up and do something to address a behavior. I've been in homes and heard moms shout, "Don't touch that! Don't climb up there! Don't throw your Cheerios!" to kids who obviously never pay any attention to the sound of their mother's voice. But I get it now: yelling is always easier than doing.

Doing means getting out of your chair, walking over to the pumpkin, and tenderly correcting the same disobedient behavior for the twenty-seventh time. It's tiring and boring, and moms are worn out, so they yell or eventually just check out. By the time my fourth one was a toddler, I totally understood why moms give up and kids end up climbing into windows, where they get stuck between the glass and the screen—so stuck, in fact, that the window won't budge, forcing someone to climb a ladder, cut a big hole in a perfectly fine screen, and retrieve the toddler whose mom was too tired to get up and remove the defiant little rambler.

That curious toddler was my now-grown-up friend Sam, a third-born, attention-diffused kid who drove his mom crazy. My college pal has actually turned out to be a really great man after being such a dorky, noncompliant kid. God bless his mama, and God bless us, the moms who can't yet see that their kids are probably gonna be OK. But in these years, we have to do more than yell. We have to be the "boundary moms."

A boundary mom gets up and crosses the room to discipline disobedience. It's harder. It costs time and energy and emotion. But we don't really have options. Those little hearts matter too much, and we have to be the adult who is too smart to resort to yelling.

Similarly, we have to involve ourselves in determining the boundaries that keep preteens and teenagers safe. We must hold the lines of sanity and protection, and if we do, the statistics are in our favor: they're going to make it.

A good parent is supposed to create a safe place for her kids to grow up. That means we make boundaries for their physical safety, their emotional health, and the general, day-to-day creation of good character inside their hearts. We care for their souls, guarding the tender, little people they are right now and the amazing grown-up people they have the capacity to become. We hold them back, inching out the lines we've drawn around their potential, until one day, all the lines are erased and the whole wide world is theirs for the choosing.

the meanest mom in the world

In our culture, and in these ridiculous, indulgent times, being the boundary mom might just be one of the most difficult things you and I will have to do. The boundary mom isn't always the popular mom. We are faced with times of personal doubt and plenty of opposition from our kids, their friends, even the parents down the street. And sometimes the boundary mom will get "the look." You know what I mean. It's that squinted, evil eye that peers across the kitchen table and says, *You are the meanest mom in the world.*

I love the old Mark Twain tongue-in-cheek quote about child rearing: "When a child turns thirteen, put them in a barrel and feed them through the knot hole—when they turn sixteen, plug up the hole." Sometimes our strong boundaries must, to a child, feel much like a rotten barrel. And it is never easy knowing when to plug the knothole and when to pry open the slats. There is no one way of creating boundaries that work for each child. Everyone is so different. And that makes our job harder.

Being the boundary mom might be one of the most important things we have to do, but it's also the thing that can take you right to the mat, screaming to your kids, "I give up! Just live any way you want. Hope that lazy, rebellious thing works out for you!" We all know that parenting makes you bushed, and boundaries require strength, many times more strength than we believe we have.

Sometimes, while speaking at a teenage girls' event, I'll say, "I am going to tell you about some of the strong boundaries I have made around our home, some of the things I am doing to protect my children. When I'm done, you are going to go home, look lovingly into the eyes of your mom, and say with all sincerity, 'I am so glad that Angela Thomas is not my mother.'" The girls all laugh, but I cannot count how many have said to me after the event, "I wish my mom had been like you. I wish she had been stronger. If she had just said no to me, even when I pitched a fit and screamed like a baby! My life would be so different if there had been stronger boundaries."

And then again, I don't know how many moms have slipped a piece of paper into my hand, asking me to write a book on child rearing. The last one I received said, "I don't know how to mother as you describe. Please write a book or teach a seminar. Help! My kids need me to be a boundary mom." I don't know if I have enough for a book, but how about a chapter to start?

Before we dive in, I want you to know that being the boundary mom does not mean becoming a legalistic, rule-keeping, ledger-toting, punishment-giving mean ol' mom. I am hoping and praying that what I do to safeguard my children is done with compassion and grace, that I talk to them enough to help them understand my reasoning and my heart of love. I have been angry, but I don't make or keep boundaries out of anger. And every time I can make the boundary a little fun, I always try to do so.

So before you yell one more time to one more kid about the same old thing you always yell about, let's take a few steps back and build a strong boundary for his or her protection and discipline. Then hold the line.

my boundary-mom lessons

SET BOUNDARIES, BUT BE WILLING TO MAKE EXCEPTIONS. When you make boundaries, you are setting up some guiding principles for the purpose of keeping your family safe. After you've done that, then you have to use your common sense and God-given wisdom to discern when a situation falls into the "exception to the rule" category. Things happen, situations arise, kids make mistakes, and moms do too. Sometimes tenderness matters more than keeping a rule.

Our kids need to feel what real forgiveness feels like, hear what mercy sounds like, and see what a place of rest and lavish love looks like. So set good, wise boundaries, and then stand on your decisions with great affection, willing to be redirected by God and reasonable with your children.

DON'T WORRY WHEN THEY TEST THE BOUNDARY. I think kids just need to push up against the boundary every once in a while to make sure it's still there. And truly, I believe it gives them security when they test the boundary and find it's still strong. I will allow a couple of tests, like when Taylor asks the same question, but in a different way. I'll let her ask twice, maybe three times, but after that I make it clear that the testing needs to end. More than one time I have told her, "One day you are going to make big money for this. People pay attorneys four hundred bucks an hour to ask the same question fifty different ways. But today, you are not an attorney. You're still my kid, and if you use that trial-court approach one more time, you will be stepping over into disobedience. The judge is about to rule you out of order and send you up the river for contempt."

You are sure to feel an occasional testing. In those encounters, the kids need to experience your strength.

CREATE A HAVEN. Our homes have to be the safest places on earth for our kids, because the home we make for them is the place where their hearts will be fashioned and their dreams will be sown. If I could write in ALL CAPS here without totally offending you, I would. This matters. Especially as single moms, the idea of creating a haven is huge. Most of our kids have to pack overnight bags way more than anyone should ever have to. So the home *we* provide has to be a refuge—a safe place to fall and the place you can't wait to get back to.

Your kids are probably like mine: they like to eat the same things over and over. Mine like the *same* mac and cheese, not some other recipe or weird casserole version of mac and cheese. They like it the way they like it, and most of the time, that's exactly how I make it. Experts say that kids choose the same foods over and over because it gives them security. But we can do more than just serve the same mac and cheese. Just think what we can give to their characters if the place they live is a homey, peaceful environment, a protected harbor that provides security and real, unconditional acceptance. A home like that would be the best place on earth for silly little kids to learn how to become amazing adults.

It's the responsibility of every mom to create and protect the haven, the sanctuary, where her kids live. We must build strong boundaries around this place where they lay their heads and do their homework. A "haven" means that goodness happens there. Evil and all its various incarnations will not be allowed.

But each of us has a target on our backs, because not only does Satan want to discourage, he wants to steal, kill, and destroy. Satan wants my kids. If you are under twenty-five, I think the target on your back is triple-sized and flashing neon. Unfortunately, grown-up women know it's true: the wounds suffered early, like choices made during junior high and high school, can leave you with a lifetime of pain and repercussions. Poor choices not only come with consequences, but they can taint future relationships, a marriage, and how our children will parent their own children. It's mandatory that we take these years seriously and do whatever it takes to build the boundaries around our havens that will protect their hearts.

I am right smack-dab in the middle of these crucial years with my four. Sadly, we have outgrown Lego buildings and tea parties and the time when I knew exactly how many peas they ate for dinner. I remember when a boundary meant fast-forwarding through the wolves in *Beauty and the Beast* so Taylor wouldn't have nightmares.

Animated wolves are long gone. Now the wolves are real people with evil intentions, cyberinvasions that pop up when you least expect them, and the mistakes an innocent child can unintentionally make in our immoral world.

Today I can report to you that my children are all in a very good place, but I don't take that for granted. Anything could happen. One of my kids could choose poorly. As a matter of fact, one day you might overhear someone saying, "Did you hear what Angela's kid did?" I have no idea what is in front of us, but I can promise you this: if Satan comes to get one of my kids, he will not come in the front door, because that's where I'm standing. He will have to sneak up through a crack in the floorboard, but he will not be allowed to prance arrogantly into the haven—not on my watch.

Right now I'm seated in my writing chair in the study. It's in the middle of the house, downstairs, where all the action is. I'm working, but I can say hello to everyone and keep up with what's going on. It's a beautiful day outside, and the kids have been running in and out with their friends all day long. Taylor is in the backyard, throwing the football with two really great guys from her school. They have been hanging out here for a couple of hours. AnnaGrace is upstairs with Rachel, our neighbor from down the street. They have been in and out the front door over a hundred times, it seems. Grayson and William mowed the yard while all their neighborhood friends watched and helped. After that, they played baseball for a few minutes, and now the posse has moved down to Zach's for a little slip-and-slide. I tell you all this because I want you to know that keeping watch over the boundary means you have to be around, engaged, and accessible.

I work at home, so I have a bit of an advantage keeping up. But many of you work away from home, so keeping up with your kids' comings and goings will require more creative solutions. Still, I am convinced that children don't need to be home alone for an extended time. Perhaps after-school activities can fill the time you're away from them, or maybe a neighbor can care for them until you can get home. I realize that making extra arrangements can be extremely difficult, but these are the years in which habits are formed and character is shaped. We have to stay in touch and committed to their care.

Making the home a haven means that I am engaged in the lives of my children. Where they are, with whom, for how long. We have conversations about what they did, how they feel, and what other kids do. I'm sure I don't get all the facts. But every time they run into the house and yell, "Mom!" I try to be ready to interact, look into their eyes, and read their countenances as only a mom can.

The next few lessons come from my desire to make my home a haven. They may not be decisions you are willing to make. That's OK. My prayer is that something I say will prompt you to create strong boundaries that keep your kids safe and the home in which they live peaceful and fun.

PROTECT YOUR FAMILY TIME. We do not schedule extra things on school nights. We may run to the store for something the kids need for school. We attend ball games or school activities in which they participate. And the older ones go to youth group or Young Life. But we don't run around endlessly on school nights. I don't drag them through the mall or out to run errands that we can do on the weekend. No sleepovers on school nights either. I don't serve on committees or go to meetings that would take me away from them at night. Balance is the goal. If I feel that we're lopsided either way, doing too much or too little, it's my job to rein us in or ramp us up to restore order and peacefulness.

NO INTERNET. NOTHING. ZERO. ZILCH. I realize this may already seem extreme to you. And for me, it's an extreme measure that goes against our culture, but my intent is not to be extreme; I just want to protect my kids. As you can imagine, I did not get to this decision without a scary lesson.

Several years ago, when Taylor was beginning junior high school, I let her have an e-mail address and use my computer after school to IM her friends. As you know, kids add names to their IM lists, and most kids add all their friends' buddies until they have so many buddies that they don't even know who all those people are. One day, I read a couple of messages that had been sent to Taylor by someone she didn't know. To say they were inappropriate is an understatement. And even worse, Taylor had replied. When I asked her about it later, she said she had no idea who that person was. She was sorry she had read and replied to the questions some whacko had sent to her. I was sick to my stomach. Only a couple of lines had been exchanged, but someone had invaded not only my home but my kid's mind with garbage that I couldn't undo.

There was already a filter on the Internet, but a filter doesn't guard against this kind of interaction. Taylor was disciplined and lost computer privileges for a while. When I returned her usage, I set limitations but realized that, over time, they were really difficult to enforce, and things happen that she doesn't even mean to read or see. The language other kids use can be slimy, with sexual innuendos woven through everything. It wasn't necessarily Taylor or her close friends but other kids who get in on the messaging. I decided I was done. These years are too precious, and their minds just don't need more junk to cloud their choices. They have the rest of their lives to act grown-up. I took away the Internet completely. Really. No Internet. No e-mail. No instant-messaging. No MySpace. Nothing.

If one of my children needs to do a report on penguins, then I sit at the computer with him or her beside me. We do the research, and I print out whatever information and/or pictures are needed to complete the assignment. It's harder to do it this way, but the school won't respond to my e-mails about returning to the old Encyclopedia Britannica down in the library for reports.

Many times women want to tell me about the great filter they have on their computer to protect the children. I hear you and I believe you. But my friends with teenage sons who've become addicted to pornography had filters too. Their friends at school taught them how to get around the filter.

They have the rest of their lives to become Internet savvy, so for now, no Web for my kids. Besides, I still think kids should play outside.

SET SERIOUS GUIDELINES FOR TELEVISION AND MOVIE WATCHING. My kids rarely see anything that comes on TV after 9 p.m., mostly because we go to bed by then, but also because there isn't anything any of us needs to put in our heads after 9. And even before 9, it's little more than *American Idol*, *Extreme Home Makeover*, or the Disney Channel. We have cable, but my television allows me to hide the channels I don't want my kids to flip past. We also only have one TV, so everyone who walks through the room knows who's watching what.

My kids love movies, so I try to get them to everything that's appropriate. We mostly see PGs, some PG-13, but obviously no R. The other day Taylor (now sixteen) called and asked to see a PG-13 movie with her friends. I hadn't heard of it, so I pulled it up on www.pluggedinonline.com. It was a teen movie, probably with some lame story line, but mostly it seemed to be about girls trying to get a guy, wearing bikinis, and making a lot of stupid teenage sexual mistakes.

I called Taylor back and said, "Honey, I know that the ratings system says that you are old enough to see this movie, and by their standards, you are. But it seems to be about a lifestyle that you don't lead. I just don't see the point in sitting through a movie that makes you feel like a nerd for not taking your clothes off for some guy. I'm sorry. I don't want to be the mean mom, but I'm voting no."

And then my amazing kid, to whom I try to give a lot of privileges, said without the slightest hint of disappointment, "It's OK, Mom. We'll just see something else." And they did.

Same thing goes for video games. My boys love their Play-Station and Nintendo games. But I only allow E-rated games in the house.

One afternoon a visiting kid had a whole stack of games he was bringing over to play. I stopped him in the garage and said, "Hey, let me see what you've got." He was proud to show me his games—until I took out everything not rated E and said, "If you don't mind, we'll just leave these here in the garage until you go home. If it's not rated E, it's not going inside." Of course, he looked at me like I was a dork, but violent games that promote evil are not coming into my haven.

Maybe you feel you have already allowed too much with regard to movies, video games, and television. I still think it's really OK to sit your kids down and say, "I have decided to make some different choices for our family. None of these new boundaries are because you guys are bad or have done anything wrong; I just want to keep us protected."

As you already know, the rest of the world isn't so worried about what their kids watch. You will be unlike most of the other parents, but I'm praying our kids will turn out with beautiful hearts, because while they are growing up inside the haven, they don't have to filter out the trashy and violent messages that run counter to the values we're trying to build. The way I see it, they can balance all those messages later, but for now, in the growing-up years, I want to give my kids the gift of steady, well-adjusted protection. Sheltered, no doubt, but growing up sheltered actually worked out great for me.

NO POKER NIGHTS FOR MY PRETEEN BOYS. I have nothing against the card game of poker. As a matter of fact, a lot of the men I know enjoy it. And all of those men also bet, albeit relatively small amounts, on their playing. But they are grown men, who are willing to pay, literally, for the consequences of their own choosing. They are also aware, I hope, of the signs of addiction and its devastating effects.

Now, to my boys. I am absolutely certain that, at this time, my nine- and twelve-year-old boys don't need any gambling training from other preteen boys. Gambling lessons in elementary school seem ridiculous to me. But you'd be surprised how many other parents disagree. And that's OK, but I have drawn what I believe to be a common-sense boundary. If my boys want to play poker with their hard-earned money when they are adults, then they will. But for now, inside the haven, we won't be rolling out casino night anytime soon.

PART-TIME JOBS, A DRIVER'S LICENSE, AND OTHER GROWN-UP THINGS. Wow. I have one in the second grade, one with a driver's license, and two more just chomping at the bit to be older, sooner. In many ways, it's time to enlarge the boundaries. My oldest one is ready, and I believe her heart is too, but I am still not willing to strap her into a rocket and launch her out toward the great unknown. I am expanding Taylor's territory, but slowly, sometimes to her chagrin, over time, with oversight.

Taylor wanted a job, and I really wanted her to have one. So a few weeks ago, another mom drove her daughter and Taylor around to several retail locations to get applications. Evidently their last stop was at a great restaurant very close to our house. And much to the girls' delight, the restaurant wanted to hire both of them for hostess positions. In a couple of days, Taylor received a phone call and got the official job offer.

I didn't want to feel hesitation, but I did. Taylor's friend accepted her offer immediately and began work that week. I still couldn't get comfortable with the position. I ended up saying to Taylor, "Baby, I know you're not going to like this, but I'm going to say no to this one."

"What? Mom, it's a great restaurant. The people were so

nice. The manager is hilarious. It would be so fun. My friend works there. Come on."

"Tay, you are only sixteen, and you are pretty. You'll be standing beside a bar night after night, where people will come to drink. You will have to work until 10 p.m., and sometimes later. I just don't want you to have to field the comments and conversations you'll encounter. It's just not time. If you were older, I might feel differently, but you are not, so I'm not going to let you take this job."

"Mom, that restaurant is a classy place. People won't come there to get drunk," she insisted.

Smiling at my cute, ticked-off teenager, I answered, "Sweet T, I love that you are such an innocent goofball. You have no idea where people go to get drunk. The answer is no. You'll just have to look for something else."

I knew I had made the right decision, but I felt awful. My saying no went directly against the decision of another parent I respect and love. Taylor wanted to begin working. She was really bummed. But I stood on my decision with compassion, and I prayed, "God, please give her a great job."

About a week and a half later, Taylor came floating home. She and another friend had spent an afternoon going door-to-door at the retail area near our house. At a healthy-food bistro, the owner interviewed Taylor on the spot and gave her a waitress job. She was elated. Turns out that (a) she'd be making twice the money in tips, (b) there is no bar, (c) the bistro closes each evening at 6:30, and (d) they're closed on Sundays. An absolutely perfect job for a spunky sixteen-year old girl who loves talking to people. I think I was even happier than Taylor, grateful that my boundary "no" led to an even better job than she could have hoped for. God hears these boundary prayers, and I have seen with my own eyes how lavish His answers are.

We have also stepped into the driver's license years. For a million reasons that you and I pray about, the privilege of driving alone is also rolling out slowly. Going back and forth to the grocery store. Calling in before she leaves. A two-stop errand the next time. The whole big adventure of driving *is* coming to her—just not immediately. The privilege is earned. It is obviously slower than she would hope, but I have to go with my gut. Maybe slow will save my daughter from something awful that no one ever meant to happen.

● ● ●

As I said earlier, being the boundary mom usually takes you out of the running for Most Popular Mom. Truly, I couldn't care less. I really don't mind that some kid at school might think I'm a nerd. All I ask myself is, *Are my kids safe? Are they protected? Am I doing all I know to do to take care of their tender hearts and minds?* My esteem does not come from what other kids mumble or don't mumble under their breath. I want to love all of the friends in my kids' lives, but their liking me is not necessary. I have to answer to God for these four. I am much more concerned about what God thinks of me as a mom.

We are going through a big transition in our family. My kids' dad recently moved to another city a few hours away. I think they feel as if the earth is moving underneath them. They're unsure and afraid, and they're questioning what the future holds. Several of my pastor/counselor friends told me that the best thing I can give them right now is a strong sense of security and strength. And it's true. I have seen that, in their tender moments, the best thing I have been able to give to them is my strength. And in their acting-out moments, fueled by uncertainty and anger over their state of affairs, the best thing I have given to them is an affectionate strength. In either case, if they push on the boundaries, they're still strong. The ground is not shaky here. Nothing is moving. All is as it has been. Sameness is valuable to them right now. It gives them rest.

I remember a line from an old Twila Paris song: "Deep inside this armor, the warrior is a child." Sometimes I feel like a child who'd rather have someone else make the hard decisions. It's rare to feel strong and secure, completely confident from circumstance to circumstance. On the inside, most of us don't feel strong enough to be the boundary mom. But as we close this chapter, may I give you one more piece of advice?

Fake it when you have to.

Seriously, just fake being strong when necessary. Do the next right thing for them, even if it's beyond the courage you truly possess. Sometimes I am scared to death, but if I'm not the boundary mom, no one else will be.

groovy mom

I was dropping the kids off at school one morning and would be returning in a couple of hours for a party in AnnaGrace's kindergarten class. Before she got out of the car that day, she came up to the driver's seat to give me a kiss and said, "Mom, when you come back to school today, be a groooovy mom, 'kay?"

"OK, honey, I'll be a groovy mom."

AnnaGrace wanted the best of me to show up for her party, the groovy mom who is fun and tender and nice to have around. She wanted the mom who dances and tells jokes, the grown-up who is trying to live an awake, passionate, others-centered, *grooooovy* life.

I went home that morning and put on my grooviest jeans and grooviest shoes. My baby wanted a "grooovy" mom, and she was going to get all the groovy I could find. Cute on the outside, fun and lighthearted and mature on the inside.

Now I remind myself all the time, *Be the groovy mom today.*

• • •

I used to think my life was about me. Thank goodness, I eventually came to my senses. It hasn't ever been all about me.

It hasn't ever been all about you.

The groovy, grown-up women know that.

Becoming a grown-up mom can take a while, because growing up requires us to come to our senses. I realize that coming to your senses can happen in a moment, but for me, more often than not, it has been a slow unfolding over time, bit by bit, season to season, until one day, amazingly, I finally get it, or an important life truth finally gets hold of me.

After my divorce, I was so about my pain, my disappointment, my failures, my future, and my brokenness. I guess everyone who goes through it does about the same thing. In that kind of heartache, we turn inward. I was all about me. Embarrassingly, now, I remember conversations with friends that never addressed *their* lives or *their* families. Probably for several years, I was always self-centered and focused only on myself and my ongoing crummy circumstances.

Obviously, I had a lot to walk through, but I also needed to come to my senses. It wasn't ever just about me; it has always been about the children too. It was a growing-up day when I finally realized they had to come first. These years have to be centered on their hearts and their needs.

What do they need from me right now? They need me to

be the best mom I can be. Not perfect, but consistent. Becoming stronger right before their eyes. A gentle countenance. Lavish with my love. Focused outward, toward them, instead of inside myself, squinting through my pitiful disappointment. They need me to fall into the arms of God, receive His healing, hear His promises, trust in His provision, and then stand up to love them well. Your kids need that too.

Maybe the biggest hindrance for me has been a private, internal waiting game: waiting for someone to come along and rescue me. I've been waiting on a man. We'll talk more about that in another chapter, but for now I'll just say that I have kept my life on hold, secretly hoping someone would show up and take care of us all. That means the children have been on hold all this time, too, maintained while their mom was distracted, waiting to be rescued from these huge responsibilities.

But one day it finally hit me: What if I lay the wishing down? What if I just try to love my kids well and build a great life for us? What if I spend my energies doing the best I can instead of hoping for someone to "save" us? Everything began to change when I decided to focus outward on them and inward toward becoming a groovy mom for all of us.

To me, "groovy mom" means that I am wide awake and tender toward my kids, trying to be a good mom in these years instead of wishing the time away and hoping for a different life. The groovy single mom is living instead of pining for something different. She is engaged and honest and working toward emotional health for her family. Maybe she is slicing cookies off of a log instead of stirring them up in a bowl, but she's in there, caring about her family and making it as fun as possible

Maybe I looked the same on the outside, but after the groovy-mom commitment, there was peace on the inside—you know: the I-am-making-a-good-decision kind of peace. Waking up to these years feels like the most right thing I can do for all of us. The path of least regrets. Focused on family love and home building.

Maybe you and I will enjoy romantic love again someday. I hope so. But for these years, what if we commit to becoming the best kind of mom we can muster, an emotionally healthy, stable, loving, and unselfish mom, just for them? Just think what great people they will become now that we've come to our senses and realized it's really all about them.

my groovy-mom lessons

NEVER STOP BEING AFFECTIONATE. I try never to let one of my children walk past me without touching him or her in some way. I touch his head or pat her back or kiss my baby on the cheek. Why? My kids are getting older, and I don't want them to forget being touched by their mom. Even if they are grumpy or we've had a disagreement, I touch them tenderly. They have to believe that my love for them is consistent and without condition. I don't sulk at them or reject them or ever move away. I am always moving in. Holding and snuggling. Pushing through the inevitable pouty days and stiff hugs to give a mother's love.

Grayson is in middle school, so in front of his friends he gets a tender knock on the head or something not so mushy. But when the friends are gone, I am his biggest fan, hugging him and telling him what a great man he's going to be. Taylor is sixteen, yet—this is amazing to me!—when I visit her school, she sits in my lap. She always kisses me hello and good-bye, wraps her arms around me, holds my hand at church, and walks arm and arm with me through the mall. A part of me knows this affection comes from her redeemed heart. The other part of me knows that I never stopped touching her and that affection got us through the nerdy middle-school years and into this beautiful, warm relationship we have now.

I am not saying that Taylor doesn't get frustrated with me, like when I won't let her drive somewhere. But the consistent affection seems to buffer our differences and smooth out the rough spots, where I am the boundary mom and she is not yet as old as she would like to be.

Once, I was writing an article for a magazine about raising your teenage daughter. I asked Taylor what advice she had for moms. One of the first things she said was, "Sit on your daughter's bed at the end of the day. Brush her hair. Be in her space sometimes, and don't act uncomfortable being there."

Tender affection creates security in our children's hearts. It makes home feel safe. And Mom feels like someone you want to be close to, not hide from. I don't care how old they are; figure out how to love them with appropriate, tender affection.

PLAY WITH YOUR CHILDREN. I am not a "crafty" mom. My mom is a super-craft-mom extraordinaire, but somehow it skipped right over me. So I am not great at crafty-play, like making things or building things or drawing things. Just letting the kids dye Easter eggs is a production for me. Everyone has his or her own egg-dyeing station, plenty of newspaper to protect the kitchen, and an assortment of stickers/pens/decorating stuff to give variety. And *they* do the work! I just stand over them, like the craft teacher at vacation Bible school, fretting over the possibility that an egg will fall to the floor and crack to smithereens. Then, heaven forbid, one kid will be left with five eggs while the others have six. Is there any wonder I feel stress the whole time? Most moms do stuff like that with one eye closed, yawning. Crafty just follows them around. Things like scrapbooks and Christmas ornaments are no-brainers. Mega craft stores—you know, those big ones with packets of beads and an assortment of glue guns—make my stomach hurt. I am just totally out of my element in there. I am a crafty-mom wannabe.

So I had to learn to play differently with my kids. I love to pitch. So I am maybe one of the best baseball-throwing moms in my county. The boys will run in the kitchen with my glove, knowing I'll drop anything to pitch in the backyard. It's also hard to resist a nighttime game of Uno on the bed or a great puzzle spread out on the table.

I know you don't have time and you're wasted by day's end, just like me, but we have to play with these kids. Look how old they already are. There is nothing, hands-down nothing, that means more to my kids than when I play with them. You need to play too. They need to feel your warmth and hear you laugh, really laugh, which brings me to the next lesson.

LAUGH. A couple of years ago, I hadn't gotten dinner pulled together, so I put the kids in the car and we ended up at one

my single mom life

of those bread company–type places for a bowl of soup. After we ate, we talked at the table for a while. One of the kids started quoting lines from the movie *Finding Nemo*. They were really good at running these loooong series of lines, and it cracked me up. We laughed that night until tears ran down our faces. My kids loved hearing me laugh that hard, so they wouldn't let it stop. I think they loved that I was enjoying them fully. That restaurant became special to us because of that one night. My kids think it's a great place to eat, but what they remember most is that it's a great place to laugh.

Taylor says that kids know when their parents are just giving them the obligatory laugh. She also says it makes a kid feel dumb. I've done that too much. Faked an interest. Feigned a chuckle. Who am I kidding? Certainly not them.

My family laughs more when we're all together. Dinner is good. A run out for ice cream or hot doughnuts is a great time for stories and silliness. Piling on my bed late at night can create an evening full of late-night laughter. Of course, the kids take my lead. If we need to laugh, my being grumpy could destroy the whole thing.

These single-mom years are heavy. Good grief, we could be sad for a million reasons. But the whole thing will become lighter if you'll give yourself permission to laugh with your children. Never *at* them, but *with* them. It might be new to you. They might not realize it's still their mom, the one with the smile on her face, who is doing a silly dance, but they will fall madly in love with the sound of your laughter joined with theirs. Your home won't be the same if you can all begin to enjoy one another. The memories will become precious when they are indexed by the jokes you told and the times you all laughed yourselves to tears.

HAVE PEOPLE OVER. From the first day we moved into our own place, I made it clear to the kids that all their friends are always invited to be in our home. I told them that anytime we are eating, whoever is here or playing in the yard is invited to eat with us. I don't always plan for that, and then one of my kids will run in and ask if so-and-so can eat dinner with us. I have learned not to worry about what we're having or if it's enough. The kids don't really care; they just want their friends at the table. So I start cutting everything in half and slicing up apples or bananas to fill up the plates.

A couple of days ago, I had just picked up a bag of tacos, two for each kid. (I have a book deadline, and for some reason, tacos don't seem as unhealthy as burgers and fries.) It turned out that four neighborhood kids also wanted to eat, so everyone got one taco, chips and salsa from the pantry, and some chopped-up fruit. They ate in a matter of minutes and were happily outside playing in no time. The old it's-gotta-be-perfect mom I used to be would have had a meltdown without better food to feed the kids. The new, let's-do-the-best-we-can mom was kind of impressed with her resourcefulness.

I realize that these years are financially lean for many of us. We can't spend a lot, but it's really the attitude that matters. Your welcoming spirit is what you are teaching your children. Two or three cans of tomato soup in a nice bowl with some crackers will feed a bunch of hungry boys and probably won't put us in the poorhouse. I always light candles and play soft music at dinner. My kids may act as though they don't care, but they notice, and if I haven't done it yet, they'll light the dinner candles themselves before their friends sit down to open their taco wrappers.

We also do a lot of shared meals, where families on our street just put whatever they have together. My kids go to the moon when we are having people over like that. They love it. Our dinner with someone else's dinner, and no one cares what we eat. Just being together gives my kids a sense of security and peacefulness.

There is something special about having people in your home. It teaches hospitality. It makes memories and creates a warm afterglow for the whole family. Stop worrying about the old carpets and the mismatched stainless. Just open your heart and open the doors of your home. Your children will learn to love a variety of people, and their presence will make your home beautiful.

CELEBRATE. My son Grayson is in the sixth grade this year. He also has no front teeth. His front baby teeth just never fell out, and eventually the orthodontist found that between the baby teeth and the permanent teeth were three extra teeth that no one should have. About two years ago, Grayson had oral surgery to remove the baby teeth and the extras to make room for the permanent ones to drop right in. Well, those teeth must be lodged somewhere above his eye sockets, because to this day they are nowhere near coming in.

Before this school year began, I cornered the orthodontist, looked him square in the eyes, clenched my jaw, and in my best intimidating tone said, "Get . . . my . . . kid . . . some . . .

teeth. It is not cool to be in middle school with no teeth. Do whatever you have to do; just get the boy some teeth." Completely secure in his big medical education, he said, "They're coming." It's been eight months, Grayson has braces, he'll soon pass to the seventh grade, but still no teeth.

You can imagine how my mother heart felt the day Grayson came home and announced that he was going to run for president of the sixth grade. All I could think was, *You have no teeth*, but all that came out was, "OK, buddy, let's pull this campaign together. If you're running for president, the whole family is running with you." We ran a competitive campaign, passing out different candy each day of voting week, labeled with some nifty saying like, "Don't be a nerd! Vote for Grayson." We made posters. We wrote a speech . . . but then Grayson gave the speech *he* wanted to give, not the cool, save-the-world speech I thought up. From the way he tells it, he didn't say one thing about peace on earth or school-wide fund-raisers to save starving children, just the way I had coached him. Seems like he just stood up there and said, "I'm your friend. You can trust me. Please vote for Grayson."

Finally voting day came, and I gave my son the I'm-crazy-about-you-no-matter-what send-off that morning. In the afternoon, as I drove through the carpool line, where all the kids were waiting for me, my eyes searched for Grayson. Did he win? I was afraid to know, terrified that he was going to be so very disappointed.

All the kids hopped in, and Grayson sat in the front beside me. I tried to read his face, but finally I just asked, as casually as possible, "Well, honey, how'd it go?"

He lowered his eyes and shook his head. "I didn't win."

"You didn't?" I glanced back at William in the rearview. "He didn't win," he confirmed.

"Oh, baby, I'm sorry. You really worked hard. The campaign was fun. I'm very proud of you," I said, trying to encourage my downcast son.

Grayson said, "That's just how it goes, Mom."

We drove from the school in silence, turned onto the street, then right at the traffic light. About a mile down the road, Grayson broke the quiet: "Mom, I really won."

"What?!?" I didn't want to believe him now.

"I really won!" I looked back at William, and he was grinning from ear to ear. "He really did, Mom. He won. Grayson is the sixth-grade president."

"Really?"

They all nodded and beamed.

As we came to a stop at the next light, I rolled down all the windows, opened the sunroof, and started hollering. Stuck my head and hands out the window. Did the happy dance strapped inside my seat belt. And sang the presidential theme music as loud as I could. "Woo-hoo! Ladies and gentlemen, here is the president of the entire sixth grade, and I am the president's mom!" On and on I went, just whooping it up and celebrating the victory till the light turned green.

I finally settled down to drive again and looked over at the newly elected president.

"That's why I didn't tell you in the carpool line," Grayson deadpanned.

They know me too well.

I love that my kids knew their mom would rock the inaugural celebration. I am wired for that stuff. And yet, I still feel I let too many things slide. I could celebrate them more with gestures that cost nothing: special notes on the mirror or purple pancakes for breakfast. I don't want to miss the little victories. I want them to have a celebrating mom who teaches them that life is too short to miss anything wonderful that happens to any of us today.

I told Grayson that night, "Baby, you won the presidential election with no teeth. Just think what will happen after you get those babies in. We'll take over the *world*!" Yeah, he thinks I'm a goofball, but I can tell he loves it.

KEEP YOUR FAMILY TRADITIONS. The year of my separation and divorce, I was a mess. And in my messiness, I let a lot of things go. Too many. After Christmas, Grayson's teacher talked to me in the hallway one day.

"Angela, I have been a single mom, and I know exactly what you are going through. I also know that you don't want to do anything to hurt your children any more than they already are. But I need to tell you that it hurts the children when they watch you suffer like this. It was also painful for Grayson that you didn't decorate the house for Christmas or do the usual things to celebrate that you have done in years before. He said that you didn't put up a tree or make things pretty like you used to. I know you are hurting, but you have to hold your family together. These traditions matter to them. It kind of means everything is going to be OK. It gives them security, and I just hate to see you take that away when they need it the most."

I needed to hear everything the teacher said, but I was heartbroken. I didn't mean to hurt the children more, but I knew I had. I was a total slouch that year. Presents, but barely. Fake smiles and just going through the motions. It wounded them, and I regretted causing any more pain, especially since I wanted to do everything possible to spare them.

It was getting close to Valentine's Day, and I had absolutely no money. I decided to make a heart-shaped red velvet cake because I had most of the ingredients, but it was so tight that I remember sweating the extra money for the three bottles of red food coloring. I cut out construction paper hearts and decorated the door they would enter after school. On the hearts I wrote what I love about each child. Finally, I ran leftover streamers around the kitchen, and that afternoon, they came home to an I-love-you party.

The next year, I did the same thing with the cut-out hearts. Then I heard one of the boys say to his friend, "Yeah, Mom does this every year. She always writes stuff she likes about us. It's a tradition." Go figure: two years make a tradition. But I could hear his bragging coming from a place of strength; he felt secure. So the tradition stuck. And I am adding more every time I can.

Just this past year we added a new tradition. We called it Hallelujah on the Driveway. It was our version of a Halloween party. I hate scary things, so that day has always been a bummer to me. I decided to invite the neighborhood over for taco soup that I served in the garage. The neighbors brought extra food. I draped white Christmas lights everywhere. We had two fire pits in the driveway. The kids dressed up and went trick-or-treating around the neighborhood. About eighty people came, and my kids had the time of their lives. We've only done it once now, but they would kill me if we don't do it again. Hallelujah on the Driveway is officially a family tradition.

TAKE VACATIONS, EVEN IF YOU CAN'T AFFORD THEM. Before you get ahead of me, I don't want you to spend money you don't have. I do want you to plan some time in the summer and call it a vacation. Borrow a boat. Use a friend's lake house. Redeem your discount passes to an amusement park. *Something* to convince your children they are taking a family vacation. They need the memories, and I promise that the memories will far outweigh the lack of luxurious accommodations.

Maybe the very most you can do is take a few days off work for an at-home vacation. These are the times I begin to pull every string I can find. A friend of a friend who has passes to a minor-league baseball game. Another friend who will sign us in as guests at their neighborhood pool for the day. No chores for anyone. A vacation mentality, even if you have to stay home.

The first single-mom vacation I took my children on was to the beach. My sister-in-law had rented a two-bedroom condo for her family of four boys. She told me I could come rent-free if we didn't mind sleeping on the floor and cooking all our meals at the condo. Not one of my kids minded. It was a blast for them to play on the beach, be with their cousins, and eat cheap "youth group" food every day. We made huge pots of spaghetti, tacos, sandwiches, and Rice Krispies Treats for dessert. We took pictures and brought sand home in our shoes. We've since done a beach trip with the cousins every year. There is something about all of us being together that keeps any of us from feeling so single and weird.

Once, before my divorce, I started a new tradition: I began by taking Taylor on a "ten-year-old" trip with just me. She got to choose the city, and she picked Chicago. We went to the American Girl store, ate yummy food, and took a carriage ride down Lake Shore Drive. It was such a special memory for her that I promised a "ten-trip" to all the kids. Just after my divorce, Grayson turned ten. I thought there was no way in the world I'd be able to pull that one off. But he had been talking about his ten-trip for at least three years. He had chosen Los Angeles as his ten-city. To get there from Tennessee felt impossible, but I decided to try to pull it together.

After an online search, I found two-hunderd-dollar round-trip tickets. We stayed at my girlfriend's apartment, and I pulled every string I could find and wound up with free tickets to the NBA Lakers versus Bulls game. What a great weekend we had, and except for the plane tickets, I spent almost nothing. I am so grateful that I pushed through to make that special memory for Grayson. God was good to us and really blessed the effort to make a blessing. This summer is Will's ten-trip. He has chosen New York City. We don't go for months, but I have calls out, trying to find a string to pull for a Yankees game. I'm hoping that one day when the boys are old and gray, they'll sit in rocking chairs together outside their retirement home and laugh, saying, "Remember when mom took us to that game?"

Vacations and time together just as a family are the kinds

of memories that only get better with age. I realize these may be the lean years, but make a long-term commitment.

TRY WITH YOUR APPEARANCE. I believe your kids really need this. All of us could hip it up a little. Just give a little styling effort every once in a while to let them know Mom still has it going on. They want a groovy mom who comes to the basketball game in something besides sweatpants and a ponytail, looking like the saddest, tiredest, most overwhelmed woman in all the city.

They love it when you look cute, so what if you try?

• • •

Maybe you never thought much about being a groovy mom. Sounds too radical, or you're too old, or life is too hard. If it has never occurred to you to be groovy, then maybe it's time to think about having a little fun with the people you love the most.

It's so much easier to be the boundary mom and the solo mom inside the freedom and love of a groovy mom.

So, whaddya say? You there, in the sensible shoes, it's time to get your groove on.

8

financial mom

The weekend after I moved into The Blessing, my par-ents were there to help me settle in and organize. When it was time for them to leave and we stood in the driveway, they had tears in their eyes, and Mama said, "Angela, I just don't know how you're going to make it." Then my daddy handed me a check for fifteen hundred dollars and told me, "I know this won't go very far, but let us know if you need help. We'll all try to do what we can."

I remember acting brave, so thankful for their generosity, but thinking to myself, *I have no idea how I'm going to make it either.* My life had been reduced to zero. Completely to zero in every way. I had nothing except my kids and a place to live, and no real plan for how to pay the rent each month. I had a new checking account—with nothing in it. Nothing in my "retirement fund" either—'cause it didn't exist. No investments. No assets. No support. No job. I was ultimately it, responsible for every provision for me and the children, and I doubted I would be enough.

Amazingly, it has been six years since that day, and I have never had to ask my parents for money. Still, they have given so much to help us. They have bought groceries for me when I was away. Often they have taken the kids to get shoes or a new pair of jeans. One year, they bought school supplies. I know I have worried them to death. For at least three or four years, I think they went to bed every night praying that we weren't starving. We never went hungry, not for one moment, but we were poor as dirt. I just didn't tell. My dad would ask, "Do you need anything?" And I never really needed anything. Sometimes I only had a dollar more than I needed, so it was close, but I was never *in* need.

My parents weren't the only ones who helped us financially. Other people sent surprise checks in the mail, probably not knowing how destitute I really was and how much those random gifts helped us make it. At least three times I've gone to the mailbox and found envelopes of cash from someone who, to this day, is unknown to me. My friend Lisa came by and said I needed to plant flowers in the beds. I told her flowers were frivolous and we'd probably skip them that year. The next weekend I came home to a beautiful bed of spring flowers. Her whole family had given their Saturday afternoon to plant a frivolous blessing.

I have such great friends. Some have brought extra meals over or taken us for Sunday lunch, each act of generosity coming at just the time I needed a little encouragement.

Even though I could have called friends or family if things became desperate, at the end of the day, I knew that it was just me. A real-life single mom, with four kids to raise and no nine-to-five job—but a whole lot of years in front of us.

A part of me wanted to be scared to death; the other part of me decided to step up and do whatever I had to do to take care of my kids.

really trusting god

It's one thing to say, "I trust God to take care of us." It's an entirely different thing to live that trust. I have talked about trusting God all of my life. And I believed I really had done that. But before I became a single mom, I always had somewhere to fall. I was "trusting," in a way, but usually with a backup plan in case things didn't work out. This time, there was no backup plan; actually, there was no plan at all. Somehow, I had to figure one out.

I have sought God's will and provision for almost every single day of my life. Becoming single with four kids would be no different. If I was going to start over, I was going to make the journey with God. I wanted to see God's plan unfold for us. I knew that my body was healthy, my mind was alert, and I could do any number of things to make money. But how would I make enough *and* care for the children *and* run our home? I had no idea.

So I told God I would do anything He sent to provide finances. Day after day, I prayed and promised Him that I would work hard. I would be faithful. I begged Him to make a way for me to care for us. When I became a single mom, I still had two children not yet in school. Full-time job, day care, after-school care, travel, continuing education . . . I couldn't put all the pieces together or make sense of how I could possibly be the sole provider. *God, how in the world are You going to take care of us?*

It might seem crazy to you, but even though I didn't have a plan, deep inside I did have an assurance. God had always taken care of me. I looked back at the last thirty-eight years and could recognize His provision and protection. I decided to put my full trust in His consistent faithfulness. So, each of my financial lessons has come through prayer, seeking, and waiting—often longer than any of us would ever choose.

my financial lessons

WHEN LIFE REDUCES YOU TO ZERO, GO THERE. I did not want to believe that what was happening to me was real. I probably hoped I'd snap out of it or that I would somehow be rescued from my financial nightmare. But the reality was: there were zero resources. I could have easily and stubbornly dismissed the gravity of my circumstances and gotten myself into piles of debt. I could have convinced myself that the children shouldn't "suffer" just because their parents were divorced. I could have told myself that I deserved better or that a financial windfall was just around an unseen corner. Instead, I decided to go to zero. Stop kicking and screaming on the inside and just go there and build from there. Survey the options and work as hard as I could, every time I could.

my single mom life

DON'T BE AFRAID OF LESS. I could probably raise my kids in a couple of tents, cooking over a camp stove and bathing in a stream. Thankfully, my single-mom life has never even come close to pioneer days, but those first years did require me to downsize and learn to live with less. For some reason we are afraid of less, as though it's going to hurt. I am here to tell you, less doesn't hurt. In fact, less didn't hurt any of us at all. We are all better people because of the years when nothing was taken for granted. Going out to eat was a treat. The dollar movie was the *only* movie. A new backpack was a reward. A day at the lake felt like a week's vacation.

I promise that less won't kill you. Most of the battle is in your head. Once you get over it in your mind and let your heart surrender to the truth of where you are, you're on your way to rebuilding your life.

Very practically, I decided to begin with only the basic life requirements. Looking back at my first-year records, these were my basic living expenses:

- Rent and utilities

- Essential food, gas, and toiletries

- A car payment, only because we needed transportation

- Health, car, and enough life insurance to care for the children

- School expenses, lunches, etc.

- Cell phone

- Orthodontist bills

- Previous credit-card debt

- A hospital debt for one of the children's surgery

- Tithe

My splurge was ordering the daily newspaper.

There was no entertainment in the budget. No eating out or amusement parks. No vacation, and even no savings at first. I sold our old clothes on consignment and used that money to purchase the children's school clothes. I wanted to begin this new life realistic about our actual needs and not afraid to live with less.

One of the things that never got cut from my budget was my tithe. When I earned any money, I tithed 10 percent and worked out the budget from there. I really wanted to see what God was going to do if we walked this one out according to His directives. Tithing was my way of honoring God for His provision to me. As little as we had, I can honestly tell you, I have never missed one dime that I have given.

DON'T SPEND WHAT YOU DON'T HAVE. This is the oldest financial lesson ever, but again, it is one thing to say it and an entirely different matter to live it. To protect myself from the temptation to spend what I didn't have, I decided not to have any credit cards, only debit cards. I know; some people have credit cards and pay the balance in full every month. But I didn't want to get caught tight one month and let part of the balance slide. More than anything, I wanted to get out of debt and not acquire any more, ever, as long as I live.

I hate debt with a passion. I realize there are health emergencies or other desperate circumstances where debt is required. I have even known many people who have leveraged debt to build a successful business or mode of income. But I cannot handle that kind of stress. I wanted to become debt-free and live in that freedom. I like the freedom side much better than the indebted side of life. Life is so much more fun, even with less, without debt. When I was finally out of debt, it was as if that ever-present sick feeling went with the last check in the mail. The shackles of "debt jail" were broken.

Not spending what we didn't have meant that the kids didn't get every cool thing that all the other kids had. It meant that I asked for business clothes for my birthday and Christmas presents. We took vacations with family members who let us tag along, share expenses, and sleep on the floor. Other kids bought lunch from the pool concession stand; we brought sandwiches and chips from home.

I also had to stop comparing. I couldn't look at other women my age, married and with children, and compare our life to theirs. I couldn't begin to say to myself, "I should have more at this age." If I had allowed myself to go there, we would have been doomed.

Most of my friends have comfortable suburban lives, and when my life blew up, theirs just kept right on going. It would have been ridiculous to compare or to waste my time wishing for what they had. I had to decide right then what kind of woman I wanted to be on the inside. I don't want to live bitter or envious. Jealousy eats away at the soul. So instead, I've had fun rejoicing over the blessings of my married-mom friends. Yelling a big "Yahoo!" when one of their husbands gets a raise, or dancing through their new house, truly thrilled for their family.

I am in a different place. God is taking care of me in a different way, and I would be a crazy woman to compare or try to acquire what everyone else has.

One of the best financial decisions I made was committing to not spend what I did not have.

BUILD YOUR EMERGENCY FUND FIRST. Dave Ramsey, who wrote *Total Money Makeover*, probably saved my financial life. This lesson is his, imparted to me from years of listening to his call-in money/advice show on the radio. When I became a single mom, I remembered that Dave tells everyone to build an emergency fund first. I think the man is brilliant. Getting that cash put away takes a lot of pressure off and sets you up to tackle whatever financial needs come your way.

Dave suggests an emergency fund—for emergencies *only*—between one thousand and fifteen hundred dollars to start. And the money is not to be touched if there is any other way to pay for a nonemergency item or expense. (I think I started my fund with a hundred dollars that was given to me as a gift.)

Dave also says to make minimum payments on your debt until the emergency fund is in place. I did exactly as he said, adding to the fund every time I could. When I finally had a thousand dollars tucked away, that money became a source of financial security for me. I never touched the emergency fund, and eventually, after my debt was repaid, I kept adding to the fund until it grew (albeit slowly) to include several months of salary in case anything should happen to me.

PAY OFF EVERYTHING LIKE A WILD WOMAN. I don't know if Dave would say it like that, but I'm sure he would agree. After the emergency fund, target every debt you have (he says begin smallest to largest) and do everything you can to pay it off as quickly as possible.

Becoming completely debt-free took me almost five years. That included credit-card debt, hospital bills, orthodontia, ridiculous expenses that came to me in divorce, and anything in my life that had a payment plan. I still have a mortgage, but that is different from general spending. Still, the mortgage is next on my hit list. I'm working to take that baby out in the next five to ten years.

A YELLOW LEGAL PAD WILL DO JUST FINE. Most of us think we need a financial planner to orchestrate our economic details. As a single mom, I don't have so many details, only bills to pay and debt to attack. Because I don't want to lose track of what needs to happen for us each month, I have kept myself organized with a yellow legal pad for the past six years.

Down the left side of the page I list each of my bills on a separate line and the amount due every month. Across the top, I block off every month for that year. Each time I pay a bill, I mark that block PAID for that month, with great satisfaction and gratefulness. I also keep a running balance for each outstanding debt at the bottom of the page. Those totals let me know what is still needed to get free.

The legal pad keeps me looking at the totality of my finances every time I pay the bills. I can see what is yet to be paid for that month so I don't misspend and leave myself short. That page has also become a great testimony to God's faithfulness to me. I remember staring at all those blocks at the beginning of one year, wondering where in the world all the money would come from. At the end of the year, I sat looking at each block marked PAID and wept. I worked at everything God gave me, and He was faithful to make a way to pay every bill.

The next year I wrote at the top of my legal pad "Watch God Provide . . . Again!"

PAY IT FORWARD. Getting paid on the first and fifteenth must be the coolest thing. I have no idea how that feels. The job God gave me is the most random job ever. I work when people ask me to speak at their event or when a publisher would like a new book. At the beginning of my single-mom life, neither one of those things paid very much, but altogether, with a few odd jobs, it was enough for us to make it.

Because I would sometimes go two or more months without getting paid, I learned to "pay it forward" with the bills. I would take my check, pay that month's bills, and then spread the advance or event check as far as it would go toward the next month's bills. I would actually prepay the expense, write the check, and send it in, just so I couldn't go back on my decision later.

With one book advance I was able to pay four months of

bills and used event money to reduce debt. Those four months happened to fall over the Thanksgiving and Christmas holidays. There aren't very many events during those months for speakers like me, so having all the bills paid in advance took the pressure off. Christmas presents were lean, but having the bills paid and not incurring any debt meant more to me than another gift that would soon be forgotten.

I also loved marking PAID across a few months of rent or car payments. Wow, did *that* ever make me sleep at night!

Because I'm self-employed, I wrote checks to the IRS for my quarterly payments as soon as I received an income check, for as much of the payment as I could afford at that time. I wanted that amount deducted from my checkbook immediately. Then I sent *all* of those checks at the quarter payment. No one from the Internal Revenue ever called frustrated by several tax payment checks. I guess they were just glad the money cleared the bank.

Paying it forward happened for me because I was scared to death, afraid that one day all my events would cancel at the same time and I'd be left with nothing. It also seemed like the best use of the money God was giving to me. I didn't want to waste His goodness when everything was so tight and the budget was very strict. All these years later, I am not afraid anymore. I have truly been the recipient of God's faithfulness, and those lessons have taught me to trust. But I still pay it forward with my mortgage, the orthodontist, our vacations, and other expenses that come up. We don't go on a vacation if I can't pay for it before we get there. Now it's fun to me to pay something off as quickly as possible. And it makes vacation peaceful for me too!

HORDE IF YOU HAVE TO. I always felt poor if we ran out of toilet paper. I don't know why, but running around the house, looking for one last roll of Charmin, always made me sad. Next thing you know, I'd feel sorry for myself, poor single mom, without even a roll of toilet paper or a man to run to the store and get one. Dumb, I know, but true.

My friend Lisa came over one afternoon and opened the storage cabinet in the garage. I had stuffed that thing full of toilet paper, paper towels, laundry detergent, dryer sheets, and dishwasher liquid. She yelled through the house, "What is all this doing in your cabinet?"

"I'm hording it."

"It will take you a year to use all of this," she gasped.

"I know, but I feel poor when we run out and can't afford to buy more."

"I will *give* you toilet paper if you need it," she said.

"Well, that's kind of the point. No forty-year-old woman with four kids wants to ask her girlfriend for toilet paper. Hording works for me. I have nothing in the bank, but with a year's supply of toilet paper, I feel like we're gonna make it."

"You're weird."

"I know."

Yep. Hording worked for me. Still does. About three times a year, I go to the discount warehouse to stock up on the staples that keep our house running. Don't let yourself begin to feel sad and deprived. Maybe something else triggers that dejected feeling for you. Use the pay-it-forward game to avoid your own personal triggers. These are the days when you need to hold your head up. And there's nothing like a whole cabinet full of toilet paper to make you think you can take on the world.

DO WHATEVER JOB GOD PROVIDES. I told you that after I became a single mom, I prayed and said these exact words to God: "Lord, I will do *anything* to take care of these children. If You will give me work, I will do it."

The summer after we moved into The Blessing, all my work dried up. My book advance had paid forward as far as it was going to go. There were no events on my calendar until the middle of fall. I had nothing. The kids were all out of school on break, so I was without child care during the days. As soon as I realized what was happening, I began praying that prayer again: "God, I will do anything."

In a few weeks, my dear friend called and offered me a job. I think she really made up the job just so I could have some income, but from her gracious heart, she called and asked me to work for her, six weekends that summer, while the kids were with their dad. She paid for my travel and all the expenses to get to where she was. Then she paid me more on that one weekend than I could have made in two weeks at any regular job I might have been able to locate around town. I had told God I would do anything. And it was obvious that He had sent me work when my friend called.

The only catch was that my job was unloading a truck, setting up merchandise, selling for two days, inventorying the remaining goods, repacking, reloading the truck, then traveling back home. It was physical work; I could do that. It was retail and people intensive; I could do that with my eyes closed.

But I was an author, and my advisors didn't think it would look good for me to be selling merchandise. It might hurt my career, they thought. You know, the job probably didn't "look" like something an author should be doing, and I have no idea if it hurt my career. But the people who worried hadn't prayed and told God they would do anything to provide for their kids. I had prayed without ceasing, and I know that God gave me a good-paying job when there was absolutely nothing else. I did what God provided, without any regrets.

You cannot say to God, "I will do *anything*," and then decide, "Well, I didn't mean *that*." God rewards hard work and perseverance. He pours out blessings when you humble yourself and do whatever is necessary. Honestly, it's that mentality that sets the amazing woman apart from the whiny one. The amazing woman is always learning, optimistic about the future, and willing to stoop down for the ones she loves. As long as I am on this earth, I will do whatever it takes to provide for these children. I am not above unloading trucks or mowing lawns or taking three extra jobs if that's what it takes to care for them.

• • •

Being the financial mom is a huge burden to carry. Simply put, it stinks. But it can be done. We can all learn to be savvy women, who figure out how to live with less and make it go farther than it should have.

9

a dating mom, or not

A while ago, I walked into a restaurant on the West Coast for a business meeting, and standing at the entrance was one of the most handsome men I have ever seen. He was in a suit, his tie was loose, and he had short, funky, stick-up hair. I tried not to stare, but, goodness! He was just so tall and hunky—and did I say he was great looking?

After a while he came over to the group of people I was waiting with and struck up a conversation. He asked great questions and told us about his work in the film industry and his life in the big city and his recent missionary trip to India. Wow! Of all things. I'd just been on a mission trip too! It was his fifth mission trip, and that just about sent me over the edge. He was smart, *and* he had a heart for others. And get this: he lived around the corner in a condo overlooking the Pacific Ocean. Good grief! *Pinch me; it's too good.*

We all liked him. Actually, that's an understatement: we couldn't believe the man was real. The girls were elbowing me, even as I was smiling politely and trying to put on my best intelligent, funny, you-can't-live-another-day-without-me persona. I'm sure I was goofy.

Before he left, he asked how to get in touch with me. I gave him my Web address. That's right, no phone number. No e-mail address. I am a grown-up, and he was a stranger. You can't just give your number to strangers. So I tried to be mature.

As Hunky, Handsome Man was leaving, he said to me in front of the group, "Maybe I'll just come to your hotel and stand in the lobby, waiting for you to come down so I can see you again." I'm sure I blushed, and I melted on the inside, hoping he would. We women all stood there, trying to imitate fashion models, until he was out of the restaurant. But as soon as he was gone, we fell to pieces. The women said to me, "Forget this meeting! Go get that man!" One of the guys said, "That is the kind of man who makes every other guy in the room want to crawl into a cave and die." The other fellows said, "What just happened?"

I wasn't sure what had just happened, but it was so incredibly fun. And a little magical. And it made me think I had just met an amazing man who might just be worth the time.

Speaking of time, it did go by. Lots of it. A few days. Then a couple of weeks. Finally, people stopped asking if I had heard from the man in the restaurant. Not a peep. Nothing. I just felt that sick stomachache thing you feel when you thought something went great, but it obviously didn't go anywhere. And it's a little embarrassing. Then, well-meaning people say, "He's probably a freak." He probably wasn't, but he never contacted me, and I felt like a dork.

Fast-forward fourteen months—I am not kidding: fourteen long, stinking months—and one day, right out of the blue, I get an e-mail forwarded by the woman who gets my Web site correspondence. The subject line bore the name of that restaurant, and my knees turned to butter. It was him. Hunky Handsome Man. And he wanted to know if I remembered him. Remember him? I just about hated him for being so nice to me and then evaporating.

I wrote back a couple of lines and told him not to hurry; I wouldn't expect a reply for a couple of years. He thought I was funny. I am funny, I was funny in the restaurant, and he had already missed fourteen months of funny. So I was cautious. But honestly, I rationalized him a hundred ways. Maybe he had been in a relationship when I met him last summer. Maybe he was going through a divorce. Maybe . . . all kinds of things could explain why he had taken so long to write. But now he sent me six or seven pictures of himself and wrote several long e-mails telling me what he does every day and about his heart for God. He told me that, the night in the restaurant, I had taken the room with my beauty and fresh, alive energy. I could feel myself forgiving him. He wanted to come hear me speak. I thought that sounded safe.

So I sent him an e-mail back, to tell him about my children. All four of them. I wrote, "Here's the part where you can feel free to stop writing. Four is a lot. I'm crazy about my kids. But you can bow out politely now and it's OK." He had never been married and had no children. But instead of bowing out that day, he immediately called, and we talked on the phone for two hours. I was impressed with his heart. He made me laugh. We planned for him to come hear me speak a couple of weeks later.

Then I did what every other woman in America would do: I called my girlfriends and told them about Mr. Dreamy. I also bought a new suit to speak in, had my hair freshly colored the day before, and probably didn't sleep well just thinking about how fun this man might be. That kind of silly anticipation is so exciting, but now I know why it's mostly for lovesick coeds. It makes you tired.

So the day finally comes. He calls the night before. We make plans. He calls the day of. All is well. Another call. He might be late. Something about a business crisis that sounded legitimate. More calls, and he's not just going to be *late*; we'll have to meet after I speak. Disappointed but OK, I understand. Later, another call. It's getting too late. Hunky Man says, "Why don't you go on to your hotel and call me when you get up in the morning?"

"I'm getting up early," I say, "and I don't want to wake you, so why don't you call me when you get going?"

"OK, I'll call you in the morning. Sleep well," he says.

"Good night. I'll talk to you tomorrow," I say.

And to this day, I have never, ever heard from him again.

Unless that man died in his sleep, I think that is the most blatantly stood up I have ever been in my whole life. I felt like a fool for having been so goofy about the tall, handsome man. And I had a new suit and everything.

About six months have passed, and I have a little more perspective. Restaurant Man was obviously a disaster, and God just protected my heart from further pain and my life from further chaos by keeping him away.

Grown-up men with healthy minds don't act like that. Honestly, I'm thankful for the experience. But even more honestly, the whole thing was a stunner. I mean, as those next days passed and he still didn't call, I knew in my mind that whatever he had going on wasn't really about me. We hadn't even spent any time together, and every phone call had been fun and engaging. But it *felt* as if it was about me. Whatever else it was, it was flat-out rejection, and—*ouch!*—did it hurt!

Or maybe he finally counted to four, and it scared the gracious return call right out of him.

I wish I could tell you that one bad experience was my only one. There have been other dating heartaches, but, thankfully, not that many, because I really haven't been in a serious dating relationship since I became single again. So, on that topic . . .

learning to date again

When my divorce was final, I think I said yes to every man who asked me to dinner, just to regain some weird sense of value. But that method soon lost its appeal, and I quickly decided I'd rather be home in my gym shorts, pulling weeds from the flower bed, happily humming a tune to myself, and hoping great things about the future, than sitting across from one more person with whom I knew I had absolutely no connection.

You'd think we'd know these things right off the bat, but it took me several months to learn that I could not go from the great heartache and woundedness of the previous years and expect to be a healthy woman jumping into a healthy relationship. I was such a mess, and it scared me to think of making a relationship decision from that kind of pain. So I decided not to date for a year. That year went by, and a lot of great things happened in my heart, but so much healing was still needed. So I made the commitment to not date for another year. Finally, at the end of the second year, I decided that if someone asked me to dinner and a movie, I'd go.

Through the next years, I actually had dinner with some fabulous men. Really great guys. Intellectual. Funny. Bright. But I haven't had one serious dating relationship in all this time. If I had to guess why none of these men have become relationships, I'd say that each one, in his own way, was unable to get his arms around my life and my children. So, most of those great guys just eventually stopped calling. They were either too polite or too chicken to tell me that five people were more than they could love.

When a man you enjoy stops calling, it hurts, but in this bizarre, learning way, it's been good for me to go through the disappointment a few times. Even the hunky, big-city man who forgot to call me back the next morning has been a part of my growing. I have learned a lot. I have been protected from becoming comfortable with someone and then making a marriage decision just for the sake of comfort or convenience. Inside of me, there has been a personal wrestling over dating. But I know that sorting-out process is making me stronger and wiser.

I have come to know a few things for sure: One, this is the

best life I have ever known. I am in a good place, and I am not desperate. I'm very content to wait for a very good man with a very big heart. Two, I haven't met the companion I have prayed for yet. Not one of the men who forgot to call back was The Man. He is still out there. And three, even if I don't meet someone for another ten years, my heart is full of anticipation for the companionship. Until then, I am committed to becoming an amazing woman with an amazing life.

I have plenty to keep me busy. Kids to raise. A home to make beautiful. A heart that wants to enjoy every single day and pay attention to the blessings. There are people to serve and a great, big world to see. I'm not waiting to live while I wait on *his* love.

Ultimately, I have become more and more OK with this no-amazing-man-relationship place that I'm in. I actually think it's working out better for me and for the children. And I have almost convinced myself that it could be to our advantage to raise the children alone, without the issues of stepparenting and blended families. If I meet someone to share my life with *after* they are grown, that will be whipped cream piled on top of this great life that we already have together.

But it would be wrong of me to mislead you. I have been designed feminine. I long to be held. I desire to be desired by a man I desire. I would love to be cared for. I get tired of being strong, and it stinks like everything to make major life decisions alone. I was made to be loved by a man. I know that. I own it. But for now, it's just not so. I am in no hurry, but I would be lying if I didn't tell you that it would be so great to have someone to share a meal with, or a movie, or a phone conversation at the end of the day.

So my dating lessons have come in a clumsy effort to find balance. Many have come in heartbreaking moments, some because I finally became brave. But I'm happy to report that I am not mad at men. I enjoy them very much, and one day it will be fun to love one man well. Until then, I'm just trying to date well and enjoy each interaction and each moment.

my dating lessons

YOU NEED TIME TO HEAL. Maybe you don't need two years, as I did, but if you don't take the time you need for healing, you'll bring your wounded heart into another relationship. You could expect the next man to be the answer, setting yourself up for more disappointment, and maybe even hurting your children in the process.

If you make a commitment to heal apart from dating, then one of the biggest distractions to your heart's recovery is removed. You get to find out who you are, and who you are meant to be, without being lost in the next relationship. You won't struggle with concern about what *he* likes, maybe even hiding your true self, just to hold on to his companionship.

Taking some time off from dating isn't going to hurt anything, and I am certain that the time away, well spent, will serve to make you better. I knew at the end of my first non-dating year that I was a different woman than I had been the year before, and it scared me to think, *What if I had entered a relationship as a wounded woman, choosing as though I was desperate to be loved?* There would have only been more pain. It would have been a train wreck.

The journey toward healing is obvious in some ways, mysterious in others. One of the more obvious things is that healing doesn't happen alone in the dark. I cried many nights, alone on my bed, wrapped tightly into a ball, and aching for my heart and my children. That was grieving. Necessary. Part of the journey. But no healing ever came to me alone in the dark. Healing comes in the light. God is the Healer, and He can be mysterious. So we have to go with God, go on the path He takes us on, in the time He allows to elapse as we come into His healing. The mystery forces us to lean into God, learn to listen for His direction, trust His faithful heart, and then believe He'll make good on every promise He has given to us.

And healing really does come. For most of us, time just has to go by. Months stacked on top of months. Laying the truth of who we are and how we got here out in the open. Getting some help sorting it out. Looking at the character we've chosen or acquired and deciding how to improve the woman we're becoming.

Most of my healing has come through other people whom God has purposely sent into my life, people who care enough to call me to a higher place and who model for me great character and integrity. In these years, I have made a conscious decision to pursue healing in every place I can find it. I have sought counseling, healing friendships, healing retreats, healing prayer, and healing honesty.

You need time to heal too. Like a big, deep, cleansing breath. You also need some time to survey the future and to determine what you want in a relationship. Take it. And take time to focus on your children, look into their eyes, pour yourself into their world, and love them purely and without distraction. I think you'll be surprised by the woman you can become when you devote enough time solely for the purpose of becoming whole. Dating is ahead. But it will be so much more fun when some of the beautiful pieces of you have been picked up, rearranged, and tenderly put back together. The process of healing will make you amazing.

THE CHILDREN ARE NOT DATING. I think my kids will be shocked when they read this book one day and find out that their mom longed to be in a dating relationship but that I was hurt and rejected by some of the men I went out with. At this point in my single-mom life, about six years now, I still date in private. I refuse to parade men in front of my children. I'll go to dinner with a man on the weekends when my kids are with their dad. I'll have lunch with someone while they are at school. But I am not in a relationship, so it feels wrong to put them through my dating process.

My children would like most of the men I've gone out with. But what I've feared is that they might fall totally head over heels in love with some of them. There was this one hunky extreme-sports guy who I knew my boys would go wild about. But I didn't want to do that to them unless I was sure I was wild about him first. I wasn't, so it made no sense to hurt my boys by introducing them to Mr. Cool. See, at every turn, it's my responsibility to protect the children. With regard to dating, that means shielding them from what could feel like a revolving door. Or an occasional revolving door. Actually, most of the time for me there is no revolving, just a door that cracks open sometimes.

And I never lie to them. If they call and ask what I did tonight, and I was on a date, I'll tell them I had dinner with whomever. They usually say, "Oh," and then hit me up for a sleepover with their friends. Sometimes they have a few questions, like, "What does he do?" I answer truthfully. A few times they have even asked, "Are you dating that guy?" And I have honestly been able to say, "We have dinner, but we're not dating like *you* mean. I promise I'll talk to you about a relationship like that." They trust me. And I think it takes a lot of the craziness out of our home not to go out with men in front of them.

I look forward to the time I'll introduce them to a man I respect, with whom I have fallen in love and who will love them. Until then, my kids are not dating. They don't give me dating advice. They are the kids; I am the grown-up. I want their hearts to be protected.

YOU ARE NOT DESPERATE. Once a man knows you're desperate, one of two things will happen. If you're lucky, he'll run away from you. If you aren't, he will stick around for a while and manipulate you. Desperate women make desperate decisions with those types of men, and their decisions eventually hurt way too many people. No matter what your circumstances, no matter how lonely you are, no matter how long it has been since a man has held your hand or paid for your dinner, *you are not desperate!*

The kids and I were driving home from the beach a year or so ago. Taylor was flipping through the radio stations and came across a Saturday call-in/request kind of a show. Just then, the DJ took a call from a woman, a desperate woman.

"I'm just calling in to get you to play a song for my honey," she began. "I miss that man like crazy, and I just want him to know I can't wait to visit him on Sunday afternoon at the Alabama State Penitentiary. Honey, I love you, and I'll be there as soon as I can."

Well, Taylor and I just about lost it. And then, I am not kidding, the DJ played the song the woman had requested, and I thought we were going to have to pull off the road, we were crying so hard. The lyrics began, "She thinks I walk on water." Then it went on to say something about the woman thinking the man hung the moon and how they just don't make men like that anymore. The song is probably a fine song, but, oh my gosh, I couldn't believe this desperate woman was sending out a he-walks-on-water song to her incarcerated man up the road at the "big house."

I spent the next twenty minutes laughing with Taylor and making sure she didn't miss the point. Circumstances and disappointment might convince you that you'll have to settle for whatever kind of man you can get. You might even have moments in your life when you honestly feel desperate on the inside. But even if you feel desire at that intensity, you cannot act. You were made for more than an inmate. You are not, nor will you ever be, a desperate woman.

I was making a point for Taylor, but the lesson holds for single moms too. The radio story is ridiculous. We're all certain that we'd never be so foolish to choose from our desperation. But I watch women do it all the time. Grown-up women date crazy men who treat them badly, and all I can figure is, they must feel desperate. They'll take mean over nothing. Not me, sister. My life is too good, and my kids matter too much. We are all way past desperate.

MAYBE SOME OF US ARE NOT SUPPOSED TO BE IN A SERIOUS RELATIONSHIP OR GET MARRIED UNTIL THE CHILDREN ARE GROWN. You may not want to hear this, but the more years go by, the more I consider waiting as an option. Maybe I am supposed to raise the children as a single mom. That would be about ten more years for me to get the last one through high school, give or take. I'm expecting some to live here for longer, so you know what I mean. But that's OK, because if I stay single for the next decade, then we'll pretty much avoid all the stepparenting and blended-family issues that my friends tell me can be awful and heartrending. If we can steer clear of them during the growing-up years, then that just might spare us more therapy. The children will have my complete devotion during the time they need me the most. And they won't have yet another huge adjustment *after* all the ones they have already been through.

I'm not saying this is my plan, but I am very open to settling in and living the next years without a boyfriend or husband. My friends ask me to keep my heart open, and it is. But I also have to be realistic. I can't put my life on hold until *he* comes along. And I'm willing to consider it possible that waiting may be exactly what God has in mind.

• • •

Maybe I'll be a single mom with a date every once in a while, or maybe I won't. But the bar is set high now. I'm holding out for a hunky man. I hope you'll wait for a hunky man too.

10

waiting for hunky man

I go to a small trainer's gym at least three times a week.
One of the things I love about the place is that trainers and
clients get an opportunity to know one another. Even when I
don't want to work out, I put my shoes on and go, because I
like the people. It's also fun to have someone to talk to in
between those awful walking lunges. My trainer makes me
work harder, but it feels easier as we laugh and goof around.
Many of them have become dear friends.

At the gym, we usually talk sports and movies and "What
are you doing this weekend?" But one day last week, the conversation was me and dating. The guys get a kick out of my
stories. I am a weird-man magnet, so there is usually something funny going on most of the time.

One day one of my friends asked, "Angela, are you picky?"

Before I could get a word out, my trainer, Clayton, piped up. "Yes, she's picky."

Well, then we had to define *picky*; decide if it was a bad character trait or a good, protective quality; talk about what happens to the women who aren't picky; and resolve that *picky* doesn't mean snooty or unattainable. Turns out I'm picky. And it's a good thing. All the guys said if I were their sister, they'd want me to be picky, and they'd be mad as heck if I just settled for any old man out of convenience. They'd also be disappointed. They expect more from me. Long before that conversation, I had already decided to expect more from myself. Some might call it being picky, but I've decided to call it "setting the bar high."

You and I must set the bar high with regard to the next man. And if you haven't already done so, it's time for you to raise the bar. I don't view this as optional. As single moms, I think it's mandatory that we expect more. We have so many lives to consider. If we are going to bring another man into the lives of our children, not to mention our hearts, he dang well better be worth it. I believe there are really great men out there, but then there are some men who need to step up and improve themselves. It's a gift to be loved well. I plan on loving a great man well.

At this point, I have my whole future in front of me, and so do you. All of my commitments are to my children. The slate is clean concerning romance and my heart, and I think that's so exciting. *I* get to choose. I get to write this major motion picture called *The Rest of My Life*, and one day it will be fun to meet the hunky leading man. I am at peace about the timing.

Not in a hurry. The anticipation is thrilling. And so I pray. My next man has been prayed for, for years now. So I trust God for the right man at the right time, in just the right way.

Meanwhile, I'm having such a nice time going to dinner every once in a while. And I am trying to consciously use this time to examine my desires, balancing both the realistic and the dreamy. Observing what goes on around me. Watching how other women have chosen and how that turns out for them. Deciding what I like in a man and what I could learn to like. What matters to me most.

Years have gone by now, with so many experiences, and I am more resolved than ever to keep the bar of my expectations securely bolted on the higher pegs.

• • •

I wish we were all piled into some condo somewhere by the beach right now, having a big weekend girl party. This would be the most fun chapter to talk to you about. I would love to hear your stories and laugh over the lessons we've both learned, but until then I'll just have to tell you some of mine. I hope something I say prompts you to move the bar of your expectation. Notch it up a little. Expect more, because you and your children deserve more. Determine to become an amazing woman waiting for an amazing man.

a bunch of waiting-for-hunky-man lessons

For a woman who hasn't dated much (at least it doesn't feel like it), I sure have a bunch of next-man lessons to share.

Some of these come from experience, others from observation. I don't want to miss the obvious next time. I want to use this time to become smarter about relationships, study myself, and learn from the advice other men and women have given me. Right now, I have a meandering kind of dating life. A little date here, little date there, with a lot of time in between to think and pray and ponder. So here are today's lessons.

DON'T BE STUPID TWICE. I almost hate to start with this one, but this is perhaps the one thing I have said the most since my divorce. I would watch men and women all around me in a hurry to jump into another relationship and eventually a marriage, only to realize that they had done exactly the same thing, the wrong thing, to themselves again. We could all be stupid twice—even three times—if we don't pay attention.

I realize that many of you weren't stupid the first time. I hope I don't offend you or your ability to choose wisely the second. But there are many who don't learn from their mistakes or consider the lessons they should have learned by now.

A friend of mine told me her niece remarried. The niece had known the guy for a while, and none of her friends disliked him—it's just that they didn't really think he was the one. She had set the bar high but then lowered it for this guy. They couldn't come up with one solid thing wrong with him, but he just didn't seem right for her. All of a sudden, before they knew what was happening, the niece was married. Engaged one week and then off to a wedding chapel the next. The whole thing was a whirlwind. She said she was crazy in love. Well, who were they, the schmucky friends, to question crazy love?

My friend and her niece were having lunch one day, and she asked her, "Do you have any advice for me? Any words of wisdom now that you have been remarried for a while?"

The niece ducked her head and whispered, "Don't do it."

"What?" she asked.

"I don't mean to sound negative, but please don't do it. It's not like you think it's going to be. I was just so lonely, so very, very alone, that I thought I couldn't stand living one more day like that. Nothing is as I hoped it would be. We are miserable, and I'm not sure it will last much longer."

When my friend told me her niece's sad story, my heart broke for her. Just lots of sadness over her private pain. And then the realization that it could have been me. I have been lonely. I have continued to see lower-bar men just because they offered companionship when I was otherwise alone. I have almost jumped into a wrong relationship because I felt as though nothing else was coming. I could have been in that woman's shoes right now.

My friend's niece isn't stupid. But in a weak moment, she made what I'm sure she would now call a stupid choice. Any of us could do that. We have to be aware. We have set the bar high for a reason: to keep us from more heartache and regret. And to protect our children and our homes and the future that burns so bright for all of us.

WARNING SIGNS FROM DR. PHIL If you see any of the following signs, don't go a step further. Bells should be going off, because these are deal breakers. Hit the eject button immediately and parachute to safety.

- He drinks too much or is an alcoholic or drug addict.

- He's abusive—physically or verbally.

- He has a bad temper.

- He's overly jealous.

- He's dishonest.

- He's controlling.

- He tells you how to dress and who to hang out with.

- He has a gambling addiction.

- He says he "can't live without you" after just two dates.

- He's thirty-five or older and still lives with his parents.

- He says he's "not technically, legally single. But we've been separated a long time."

- He doesn't make eye contact when he's talking to you.

- He doesn't introduce you to other people when you're out with him.

- He isn't there for you in times of crisis.

(Dr. Phil McGraw, *Smart Love* [Free Press, 2005], 29)

YOU NEED TO LIVE IN THE SAME CITY AS THAT HUNKY MAN BEFORE YOU MARRY HIM. I know this sounds like something you say to young kids who are preparing to get married for the first time. But I think this also absolutely has to happen for grown-ups like us: the ones with kids and busy lives and houses with yards to mow and trash cans to haul down to the street. Our lives are demanding. You might be able to pull it all together for the weekend you fly out to meet the guy you've known for three weeks. But eventually you need to test-drive the relationship. You must live in the same city. Someone is going to have to get an apartment or commute or figure out a way to live near the other for several months.

Most of us can't financially afford to make this happen, but none of us can afford to make a commitment to someone we really don't know. Whether things work out or the whole relationship blows up, the investment of money and energy will be worth it in the end.

You need to know what this guy sounds like and acts like after a stressful day. He needs to see your house a wreck while the whole family is working on science-fair projects. You need to meet each other in the day-to-day and see if there is still chemistry and connection. Little weekend visits won't cut it. Anyone can pretend that long. Sometimes it's not even pretending; it's just that the contact is so infrequent that we are solely caught up in the thrill of new romance and seeing each other through rose-colored glasses. I have too many friends who found out later that their long-distance "hunks" were great for two days, but two *years* made them unbearable.

THE NEXT MAN HAS TO COME THROUGH THE DOOR HAPPY. Yes, I said "happy." *Happy* is probably a drippy word to use to describe a man. I doubt they are teaching happy at the men's conferences. I don't think I've ever heard a guy at my gym call another guy "happy." Cool, yes. Nice, uh-huh. But not happy. Sounds a little goofy.

But even though it may not be the hippest great-guy description, I'm really serious. I want him already prepackaged, before-he-gets-to-me happy. I am not saying he can't ever be sad or disappointed or grumpy. Good grief, who isn't? But at this stage in my life, I need a man who is making peace with his childhood disappointments or the rejection he has known or the failures that come to all of us. He is not moping around day after day, sad and disillusioned. I want a man who is already full of enthusiasm without me. He is stepping up and looking out at a bigger life to be lived. He is, for lack of a better word, mostly happy.

Too many times in my past, I have caught myself thinking, *If that man would let me love him, I could make him happy.* That is one of the most devastating relationship illusions ever. I have learned through some of the most heartbreaking personal lessons that a person decides in his very own little heart if he will live happy. You can add to his happy. You can multiply his happy. You can share in his happy. But you can never make someone *be* happy.

If the man you love is not already happy, then you could spend every single day, all your energies, all your resources and creativity, and still never make a dent in his disposition. People are happy because they have chosen to be. People are content and pleasant because they've done the hard work to become consistent in countenance and purpose.

Don't get me wrong. I want manly, not effeminate. A big, tall, Texan kind of presence is fine, but I don't need tumultuous, dark, mysterious, brooding, mean, obsessive, manic, or sad, the kind of guy who has been looking for the just-right woman to make him happy. I have had plenty of that, thank you very much. Let him come through the door already there. Already *happy*. To me, that's worth waiting for.

You may be way ahead of me on this one and already know you can't be the one who makes someone happy. So we'll wait together for hunky men who pulled their *happy* together before we've met them.

THE NEXT MAN CANNOT HAVE "POTENTIAL." You might think I'm crazy, but let me explain. My single-mom friend and I realized that we were rationalizing away some of the glaring, red-flag, get-a-clue-and-get-away-from-him kind of characteristics by saying that a man had "potential." We could rattle off a whole long list of reasons why he is not the man and then add at the end, "but he has potential," as if *potential* made spending more time with him OK. I think we scared ourselves when we realized what we were doing. We are both getting a little too old for potential.

If I were a junior in college and met a man who had potential, that would be different. That would be a good thing. It would mean he has strengths and gifts and a calling that could eventually become the makings of a great man if he pursues them.

At this stage in life, considering the age range of men who might be relationship candidates for a midforties woman, the next man *cannot* have potential. He has to already be there. Already pursuing his calling. Already operating in many of his strengths. Already full of vision and passion and having his own adventure. Already living an amazing life that would become even better alongside an amazing woman.

I hope you don't think this is too harsh. All us have unrealized potential that's still waiting to explode amid the right circumstances, perhaps even the right relationship. But we want a man who has already realized some or a lot of his potential. At midlife, I think it's a little foolish to fall for a man who still doesn't know what he wants to be when he grows up. Based on very unscientific observations, the likelihood of him figuring it out anytime soon is very slim.

So let the man with potential walk on by. We are waiting for the man who already *is*.

HE MUST HAVE A HEART THE SIZE OF TEXAS. There is no way to hide it and no way to downplay the obvious. At this point in my life, I am five people.

We five are a lot. We are loud and silly and busy as anything. We eat a lot and get more clothes dirty than should be allowed. We laugh until we're annoying, and every once in a while we cry. Sometimes the boys lie in the hall and loudly beg their sister to come out of the bathroom. Sometimes the girls bang on the door and even more loudly beg their brothers to save the hot water. There is always something when you are five people. Always. Always something to do or someone to love or something to endure together.

And even when I am alone, I am still five. I think for five and believe for five and fight for the hearts of five. And it can't be changed or undone or any different than it is. That's why the

my single mom life

next man must have a great, big heart of love. Strong arms that he can wrap securely around this clan. Patience and the ability to overlook the little stuff, 'cause there's so much little stuff when you are five.

Stingy men need not apply. The self-centered will be disappointed. If you ever needed to be sure that it's not all about you, then step into our world and watch life happen. Every day I am more and more convinced: it is not about me. It's about the love I give away. I want a man who can give his love away too.

He will have to be a man of compassion. He'll have to be merciful. We are a vulnerable little family. We just want to give and receive love. But our imperfections are glaring. Our humanity is frustrating sometimes. We have to ask one another for forgiveness, because it's just us. Big me and four kind-of-like-me's. All of us are just works-in-progress. None having arrived. I hope his Texas-size love gives him blurry vision. Maybe he won't be able to see what a big deal it would be to love all of us.

Obviously, he has no idea what kind of ridiculous love a party of five could wrap around him. We'll rock his world.

GO AHEAD AND BE PICKY. Most of us don't set the bar of our aspirations as high as it should be, because somewhere on the inside we've decided we're not worthy. What we hear is not necessarily a loud, screaming, *You're not worthy*! Just a little whispering lie that has woven itself through our disappointments.

The lie creeps in early. Middle school for some. High school for others. Certainly by college, we've felt the sting of rejection. Some of us have felt enough to incline our heads toward the lies, the kind that whisper, *See, you have been passed by again. You expected too much. Your sights were set too high. You are not worthy. Maybe you should just settle for the next thing that comes, or nothing may ever come your way again.*

But this time, while choosing the next man, set the bar high and keep it there. This one really matters. This decision will impact your life and your children as no other decision could.

I have a list, a real honest-to-goodness list, stored and backed up on my computer, with the characteristics of a man that are important for me. I also have my list of can't-stands; the things I know for certain that I can't live with. It's amazing how we can rationalize our can't-stands when that hunky man is being all sweet and funny. So make a list of can't-stands to read when you are silly in love and need to be reminded what you promised yourself you'd never live with.

Be honest with yourself about what you like, the characteristics of a person you enjoy, and then set the bar of your desire high, and wait. If you are crazy about traveling and never want to stop, then don't lay that down ever again. You'll die a slow death if you let yourself choose the man who wants to spend the weekend on the sofa.

I know this is ridiculous; as a matter of fact, I haven't told one person this, and now I'm telling the whole world, but there was this one man who was so wonderful—and yet so wrong for me. I had to make a "Why He's Not the One" list and look at it almost every day for months until I was finally convinced. You'd think a legal-size piece of paper, filled up completely,

my single mom life

with notes in all the margins, would be enough to convince a girl to walk away. But charming men can make you forget. You need a list.

• • •

As I began writing this section last night, I had to stop and pray about what to say to you. I knew it had to be truth. But the truth was so painful last night. It felt too intense, and I began to ache, physically hurt, as I sat at my computer. Writing about waiting resurrected the longing that I would just as soon ignore.

We can make a list and set the bar high and decide how we will love again. I have made some strong commitments to myself with regard to the next man. The people who love me are adamant that I stay dedicated to choosing well. We're all waiting on Mr. Fabulous for Angela. But saying strong things makes it seem as if you are a strong person. Some days I am. Many days I wait in strength, with my energies focused on my children and our lives together. But other days, I wait in my weakness. Yesterday, I began well but finished in a puddle. Enough years have gone by, and I should be stronger than this by now, but I am not.

It is the afternoon of the next day, and still today, I am waiting. There is no hunky man on the radar. I mean, no one. There is no man to have dinner with, not even a great friend in town to call for a movie. No one will be calling at the end of this evening just to check in and ask about my day. I just wanted you to know. Maybe you wait today, too, like me. Maybe you'd never tell anyone, because you're strong and successful and appear to have no time for a relationship, but it hurts for you too.

Even during this writing, I have prayed for him, the next man. The one out there, somewhere. The one God is preparing. I have thought of him and dreamed about what he must be like. I've tried to shake it off and go fold the laundry, do something concrete to make the wanting go away. But today I am so aware that I am waiting—waiting to be loved. And it makes me cry all over again. Then I hear the stupid whispers about my worth, and all I know to do is get down on my knees before the only One who is faithful and cry out for His mercy. His favor. His blessing. Even while I am going on to live my life, there remains the waiting to be loved.

And I remind myself that I trust God. He has held me for so long now. I trust His time and His ways. I trust His love for me. His baby girl. I trust Him for the love that is yet to be. And I promise to wait with integrity, preparing my heart, loving these kids, becoming amazing, until one day, God, in His divine wisdom, says, *Come here and look at the one I have been saving for you!*

11

turn and see

She was at least ten years younger than me, a beautiful woman, waiting in line behind several others with books to be signed. Her red, puffy eyes and a handful of tissue gave her away, as did the way she stood and her anxious demeanor. Every time I glanced in her direction, I could see a broken woman moving toward me. I didn't even have to know why. My heart ached. No matter how it comes to you, that kind of brokenness will paralyze your soul. I knew before she got to me that pain was keeping her from living. After a while, it's easy to recognize the woman you have been.

Denise spoke in a whisper, her head turned so others couldn't hear. It was a version of a story like all of our stories. She was a single mom, she had been alone for two years, and she didn't believe she could go on. She had no resources and no hope, and her circumstances had overcome her strength. She loved her children but had nothing to give them except excruciating grief over how life had turned out.

I took Denise's face in my hands. "I want you to listen to me," I began softly. "I am so sorry for every brokenness that has come to you. No one—I mean, no one—should ever have to go through the pain you have known. No one should have to raise those kids all alone. Your heartache has been great, but look at me"—she lifted her eyes—"Denise, your life is not over."

Then for some reason I took her by the hand and walked her past the line of women to the doors that led outside. It was a cloudless winter day, and a chill rushed over both of us as we stepped into the cold. I led her up a hill to the highest place I could find. And then I pointed toward a field and the place where soil met the sky. "Look out there," I directed. "Denise, it's all still in front of you. The rest of your life is waiting to be lived. The lifetime to come is probably longer than the one you have already known. You must eventually turn from all the regret and all the consequences and see that God still has a plan and a purpose. I don't want you to spend one more day in the dark. There is a new horizon waiting for you. A new path and a new place where you believed there has been none. Turn and see that God is good. Life is big. You get to live again." I held my new friend as she cried; then I prayed for her, and we walked back inside.

I'll probably never know if anything I said or did that afternoon made a difference, because turning requires a choice. I don't know how Denise decided to choose. But I do know that every time I have the opportunity, I will point a broken woman

my single mom life

toward the horizon and tell her about the God who makes broken lives new.

paralyzed

Sometimes life is paralyzing. Emotionally. Mentally. Spiritually. Something happened or a million things happened, and it feels as if you can't move anymore, as if you are held in bondage by your circumstances, at the mercy of someone to come with compassion to your rescue. I know what it feels like to live paralyzed with fear. Pinned down on every side. When the outcome seems beyond your control. And nothing you do makes a difference. There is no movement. No strength. No hope.

But the same truth holds for all of us who have been paralyzed by pain or brokenness or consequences: we still get to choose where we look. We can look down and focus on our inability to move, with the greatest of pity. We can mull over our regrets and retrace our steps back to our loss. We can say over and over again, "I am paralyzed." And there we'll be, staring at our misery as though that's all there is and all that ever will be.

Or we can turn our heads and see. Change the intent of our gaze. Move our focus. Lift our heads and look toward the horizon.

Why don't you? You can look at your past choices or your present condition, or you can turn and see that God is good. He can make a new way even if you have believed there was no place to go from here.

Read what God says to us through the prophet Isaiah:

Forget about what's happened;
    don't keep going over old history.
Be alert, be present. I'm about to do something brand-new.
    It's bursting out! Don't you see it?
There it is! I'm making a road through the desert,
    rivers in the badlands.
(43:18–19 MSG)

Today, what if you decided to turn and see God? What if you could see that everywhere God is, there is the fullness of His character and that He promises you a love that is big and deep and wide and high? He is doing a new thing with your future. He makes brand-new roads through the desert of your circumstances. His plans for you include more than you could ever imagine or hope for. The day has come for you to stop going over "old history." The future is bursting out in front of you. Turn and see. There has been a long, dark valley, but we are walking toward the mountain of God.

waiting to be rescued

Posttraumatic single-mom syndrome. I doubt there's really such a thing, but "ongoing shock" is probably the most appropriate descriptor for my first years doing this. I hadn't been planning my entrance into single momness. Neither had I read one book or talked to one other mom to find out how it had gone for her. But the day I packed the laundry baskets and put the children in the car, I became a single mom. I was as unprepared as any woman could be, and an emotional zombie besides.

Now I look back and realize that woven into the trauma of those first years was a hope, probably even a prayer. I privately wished that something—some*body*—would miraculously happen to me. That someone would rescue me from all my responsibility, loneliness, and heartache. That someone would show up to fight for me. And that someone would love me enough to help me raise the children or provide for all of us or somehow make the burdens go away.

So secretly, I waited to be rescued. I dreamed of some great man who'd pull into my driveway and say, "Angela, I have been looking for a woman like you all my life. I've always wanted four children, and I can't *wait* to love your children as my own. Do you think they'd like to go boating? I'll buy us a boat. Do they like camping? I'll pack the tents and blaze the trail. You are the most beautiful woman I've ever met, and I can't wait to show you the world. Come into my arms. Listen to me tell you how much I love you. Let me take all your burdens. You never have to worry about the house payment again. I will add your entire family to my health plan. Fret not about college or retirement or vacations. I will take care of you and these fabulous children all the days of your lives. Why don't you just run down to the mall and bring home all the shoes you can carry. I love the five of you. It's all okay now, I promise. You'll never have to worry about anything ever again."

But do you know what happens when you wait to be rescued? You put living your life on hold. You search the face of every man you meet, wondering if he is the one who will save you. And you strategize and manipulate and coerce situations and circumstances, all in hopes that something else will be the answer. Someone else will know what to do. Fear presses in. The burdens feel heavier with every step. The ability to see God grows dim. Strength is gone. So we wait. Rescue feels like the only way out.

I guess I waited at least three years. Not really dreaming or building or becoming. Just holding the fort down. Waiting for the cavalry to top the hill . . . *anytime now*. Strong horses neighing. Flags waving. Trumpets blaring. But you already know what never happened. The cavalry never came, at least not like I'd imagined. Life just doesn't go like that. Movies go like that, and novels read like that, but in real life, the one you and I are living, it just doesn't happen so much.

Waiting for rescue sets you up for incredible disappointment. People just don't follow the script you have written in your head. Very few have been brave enough to come looking for me, and when they find five, it scares them to pieces. My life is big and complex, and most people are ready for simple, with little effort required. Sadly, I get it now. Heroes are difficult to come by. Being rescued like that is for Hollywood, and I live in Tennessee.

i am not worthy

I told you earlier that after enough years go by without rescue, we can begin to think ourselves unworthy of being found. It's a ridiculous emotional path to take, but we are women, and a lot of our pain feeds the inner murmurings that tell us we have always been unworthy. Mentally, it seems to be the first place we go when things don't work out. *I didn't really deserve that anyway. Why would I think a woman like me could be rescued? My past mistakes have ruined my future. Nothing is probably ever going to turn out.* You know the kind of lies I'm talking about. And the big one keeps reminding us how unworthy we are.

God has dealt with me about thinking myself unworthy. Turns out *unworthy* is kind of the point with God. Read what I wrote several years ago:

Let's just nail something down right now. We are not worthy. We never could be even when we hoped we might. We are not able on our own. We are not good enough and never will be. We are not worthy, never have been, and never had a shot at trying. That is the whole point. That is the reason we belong to Jesus—because we are not worthy . . .

Instead of a discussion on dysfunction or a theological diatribe, God says [to us], "Let Me show you how I feel about you. Your worth is settled because you belong to Me." . . . Your value and mine comes from belonging to God. (*Do You Think I'm Beautiful?* [Nashville: Thomas Nelson, 2003, 105–107])

Everywhere I go, women want to tell me how unworthy they are. The stupid choices they've made, the consequences they suffer. The regrets. All of it. I can relate. Goodness, I don't know anyone who hasn't felt unworthy or unnoticed or unloved. All of us have been there. Full of remorse and absolutely sure our worth is gone. But God sent His Son Jesus to rescue the unworthy—that would be you and me.

God sent His only Son for an unworthy woman like me and an unworthy woman like you because His love isn't based on worth. You are His beloved. His creation. His idea. And unworthy is just a lie that keeps your life on hold. God has made a way for you and me, and the Way is named Jesus.

The woman who believes that Jesus is the Rescuer sent by God is held tight and safe inside His arms of love. I believe that Jesus came for an unworthy woman like me, and it makes me grateful. My entire life has *already* been saved. That means *all* of my life, including the past that has been forgiven by His grace. Hope still reigns.

A woman who is waiting to be rescued must remember to whom she belongs. When you belong to God, the rescue has already been made. What remains is a decision to trust the unseen hand of God more than the circumstances that cloud your vision.

So what's a single mom with four kids to do?

God whispered to me, *Turn and see.*

the better way

God had more for me than an easy way out. A cavalry rescue would have been so easy for Him. A blink. A moment. A word spoken by the Sovereign and it would have been done. He could have sent an entire regiment on my behalf. But it turns out that these circumstances are not about my being rescued again. They are about my heart and my faith and my becoming. But God had more for me when He whispered, *Turn and see.* He was coming to rescue my hope and build my character and make a way unlike anything I had dreamed. God has come with the better way.

I believe He wanted this baby girl to grow up right in front of her children's eyes. He knew they deserved a grown-up mom who is stronger now because her character has been tested and approved. Truly, I did not want this path. I did not want this different kind of rescue. I really wanted the easy way out. I tell my friends all the time, "No one should have so much character." But on the inside I am glad. I know more about faith and entrusting my heart to God than I would have ever known if the cavalry had come.

I have fought this way in my spirit. The fight was about not wanting to grow or change. I didn't want to be the sole provider. I didn't care to know anything about lawn mowers or car maintenance. I didn't want to dream without someone to share the dream with. So I put my life on pause and fought the growth that God wanted.

Maybe you have put your life on hold, too, waiting for an easy way out. Rooting for another kind of rescue. Searching for any path but surrender. Fighting in your spirit. Refusing to take up all your responsibilities. Whining because it's just you. I know; really, I do. But God calls to you too, "Turn and see."

All His amazing plans for you. The hope that He gives. The future beyond your imagining. It's all still in front of you. Even a single mom, with two kids or twelve, can turn and see that God is good. His rescue still holds. Your great, big life is in front of you. The better way is to turn and keep walking through the shadow of this valley until you are standing on the mountain of God's love.

To choose this way means that I have to give up on waiting. It is time to live the life God has wanted me to see all along. It means letting myself dream some new dreams for me and the children. Making plans that don't involve a miraculous deliverance. Stepping up to the responsibility plate—even the little things, like increasing my life insurance, making a will, fertilizing the lawn, and planning a vacation for five. It also means trusting God with more intensity than I ever had to trust anyone. Learning to lean into His promises with the full weight of my hope. Banking on His faithfulness. Really and truly counting on God to come through as I step in the direction I believe He has shown. It means that I pray and seek His wisdom. I determine to live with passion and then remain strong in that determination, resting like a baby in my Father's arms.

This life I am turning toward scares the spit out of me, and yet I am running toward the horizon of God's goodness with everything I have. The way I figure, waiting is nothing more than wasting away, and we only get to live this life once. I want to turn from my insecurity and see God and His power.

the little and the big

While waiting on whatever unbelievable thing was going to happen for me, I put almost everything on hold, the little and the big. One of the little things was my watch. While I was still married, my watch was broken beyond repair. I never bought another one, mostly because it seemed like an unnecessary purchase and money that could be better spent somewhere else. After my divorce, there was even less money and a cell phone that could tell time. I never told this to anyone, but I had decided that maybe one day a man would come who'd love me so much that he'd want to buy me a watch. Not some inexpensive piece, but something indulgent that you give to the woman you love.

As of the beginning of this past year, I was still without a watch, still kinda waiting . . . I had probably spent *eight years* of watchless waiting. But in January I was on a trip with Taylor and decided to stop waiting on love to buy me a watch. I know this is the most ridiculous thing you've ever heard, but I finally wrestled some backbone to the ground and bought one. And not only did I buy a watch, but I splurged and got exactly the kind I'd hoped some man would buy for me. It has little, tee-tiny diamonds and a stainless-steel band, and it's exactly the shape that I love. I look at that thing all the time. It's just a watch, but for me the indulgence meant more. It meant a decision to go on with my life and stop checking my cell phone just because of some hokey pipe dream about a man and a watch.

The biggie came months later. My kids and I bought a house two years ago. That was a huge step all by itself, but we had to live somewhere, and getting that house felt like a blessing right from the hand of God. Before we ever moved in, though, I began telling everyone, "I love the house, but one day we'll have to do *something* about that kitchen." You know how you buy a house in a place you want to be, even if everything about it doesn't suit you? That's what we did. We bought a great house with a narrow galley kitchen, because it was located smack-dab in the middle of all the people we love. But now, after two years, when you get all five of us in the kitchen with four or five more friends, and then someone opens the refrigerator at the same time that someone else opens the dishwasher, the whole kitchen is blocked and I want to scream.

Even before I closed on the house, I started dreaming. *One day, we're gonna push out the back wall and join the kitchen with the family room to make one big, ya'll-come, brand-new, gazillion-cabinet, gas-stove, double-oven, fancy-pants kitchen that the whole family—plus friends—can use and enjoy.* And I talked about it. And I thought about it. And I prayed about it. Bought kitchen magazines in airports. Drew little renovation plans on the backs of plane tickets. Worried and fussed and counted my money and, for the past two years, just hoped somebody would come along and buy us a different house with a big kitchen so I wouldn't have to make this decision all alone.

People look at you like you're crazy when you tell them your kids don't want to move from this very spot, so we're going to blow the back off *this* house and make it right. For some reason I don't think they'd look at me like that if there were a husband standing beside me. But without one, they do, and it makes me doubt myself. "Are you *sure*?" they ask. And I always tell the truth: "No."

Truth is, we don't need a bigger kitchen. We don't even need all the house we have now. We could live in one room if we had to. But it sure would be great, and these are the years we could enjoy it. I could have the whole youth group over anytime we wanted. I like that kind of thing. Lots of people and food and music. It just makes me really happy. So I think I want to. And folks still look at me funny.

What's hard is that there is no one, absolutely no one, to sit across the table from me, look at my ripped-out magazine pages and pencil drawings, and say, "Baby, let's build this thing. And while we're at it, let's have fun." Making this kind of decision alone has been one of the hardest things I've ever done. I finally realized that I could wait forever for someone to call me on the phone and say, "Hey, go do that kitchen. It's gonna rock, and you're going to be glad you didn't put it off."

So, more as an act of determination to keep living and growing, I called a builder, who called an architect. Then my builder said, "Angela, if you aren't 100 percent sure, we don't have to do this."

"I will never be 100 percent sure," I told him. "All the facts say build. Every calculation says it's a great thing to do with regard to investment and family. But I'm the kind of person who will probably never be sure until someone else tells me I can. There is no one. So let's build anyway."

On the table across from me, this very minute, are the finished plans and the signed contract to build a kitchen. We're waiting on a lot survey, and the builder thinks we'll pour the footings in a couple of weeks. Everyone I know is probably whispering behind my back, "What in the world is she doing now? That woman just keeps stirring something up all the time."

But it was as if the Lord said to me, *Angela, turn and see. One day these kids will be gone, and all you're gonna need is a hot plate and a minifridge. There is a difference between talking about living and really living. These are the days. Build the kitchen, and love every person who comes to sit around your table.*

I know it's just a kitchen, but the process has been a big one for me. To turn and see and then run toward what's in front of me. Wow. I can hardly believe this single mom is wearing a watch and acting so brave.

my turn-and-see lessons

TURNING IS A CHOICE. Someone said that you believe what you focus on, whether it's true or not. You are the only one who can decide if you will turn your focus from what you've come to believe, out toward the horizon where there is hope. No one else can choose for you.

Maybe you will not choose to turn. Fear will win. Life will stay the same. And all that is waiting for you to discover will remain hidden, a treasure you chose not to find. But I am praying that won't be your choice.

THE ABILITY TO SEE DIFFERENTLY IS NOT GIVEN TO THOSE WHO NEVER LOOK UP OR OUT TOWARD THE UNKNOWN. I was flying with one of the children one day. As we began our ascent after takeoff, she looked down and said, "Mom, all the houses and cars look the same from up here." I loved that. From her perspective, no one's house was bigger and no one's car was newer. There was no need for comparison with a different perspective.

Your circumstances might remain the same, but when you decide to turn and see, a different perspective might just give you the fresh vision you have needed.

LIFE WILL GO ON WITHOUT YOU. I am assuming that you are a lot like me and you've missed too much already. Not one more day has to go by. Today, you can turn and see that God is good. His promises were meant for you. And truly, the best years are waiting.

how, then, shall we live?

I hope by now that you're beginning to see—to believe—that God can make a way for you where nothing has seemed possible. I'm praying that you are turning with the intent of your heart, with the fullness of your passion, and moving toward dreaming again. If not, I wish I could take you by the hand and walk you to the nearest field to point you toward the horizon. To whisper, "Can you see that? Your whole life is still in front of you. Can you see God there, calling you toward the plans He has for you and your children? Can you hear Him saying your name and directing your steps?"

I know you are a single mom, and for some reason most of us hang our heads and cringe a little every time someone new acts like he or she is looking for the other half. It can feel as if dreaming and planning and building a life are over. We think to ourselves, *Just keep your head down and get these kids raised.* I don't know why we feel a little second-class, but we do. We can act as though we're not a whole family when, in fact, we are. We cover the insecurity by pretending. It's a weird emotional balance. Fighting to be whole, wishing things were different, trying to be brave, and marching toward God's plan anyway.

I don't know everything about this journey, but I am positive that every time God is involved, we are supposed to live with passion and purpose. I just see too many of us waiting to live. Watching. Ducking. Hiding. Smiling behind the kids.

How shall we live as single moms? I think we ought to rock—*especially* the woman who belongs to God. For goodness' sake, if we ever needed faith, we need it now. If we ever needed to believe that we have been saved, it is now. If we ever needed to live in power and strength, these would be the days. God has made a way for women like us, and it's time to take hold of everything He has in store for us.

Don't let your circumstances mislead you. Do not let your heart grow hard from disappointment. Jesus said:

> *Their eyes are blinded,*
>   *their hearts are hardened,*
> *So that they wouldn't see with their eyes*
>   *and perceive with their hearts,*
> *And turn to me, God,*
>   *so I could heal them.*
> (John 12:40 MSG)

Turn toward God. Now, what do you see?

I see four kids growing up beneath the wings of a mom who is being healed and redeemed. Four grown-ups who turned out better than anyone expected. Can you hear "Pomp and Circumstance" playing joyfully? I can. And there are weddings, and if *I* am around, there will be dancing. Grandbabies to spoil. Adventures to take. Hands to hold. And way back there, past the edge of the horizon, I see a little table in a piazza in Florence. There is a strolling violinist. Watercolor artists setting up for the day. The scent of smoke is rising from roasted chestnuts. And there is a smiling woman sipping cappuccino. Across the table is a man who is madly in love with her. He knows she is a mom-plus-four, and he thinks that makes her cool. He has seen her mended heart and thinks the beauty of brokenness is her best thing. She closes her eyes and whispers a prayer: "God, thank You for turning this scared mom away from her pain and pointing me in the direction of hope."

How now shall we live? We shall live like everything God has promised is true.

God is here. He is ready to heal and restore and make your life new. Turn and see.

One turn.

Eyes raised, squinting toward the horizon.

Deep breath.

One step. Then another . . .

Until you run.

12

love has the final say

Aldyth asked if she could take Carla and me to dinner. It had been an amazing conference weekend for all of us on my first trip to South Africa. My friend Carla traveled with me, and I had spoken seven times in about two days. We met hundreds of remarkable women, absorbed culture and history, listened to stories that broke our hearts, and prayed with the women who asked. We stayed up late, woke up early, hugged more women than we could count, and by the time our host and new friend, Aldyth, drove us to dinner that Sunday night, we had given every ounce of emotion and compassion we had come to Africa to give.

Both of us were spent. Completely empty and exhausted, and yet, we were basking in the unbelievable days we had just experienced. Great food at a great restaurant sounded perfect. I just wanted to sit and eat and smile at God over all He had done.

About halfway through dinner, Aldyth, a proper-English, South African woman said, "Angela, there is something I have been wanting to say to you."

I remember feeling anxious when she said that. Afraid that I had unintentionally offended half of South Africa with some American humor that struck them wrong. I bolstered myself in my seat and thought to myself, *Noooooooooo, not now. I'm too tired to receive correction. Just hurry and tell me whatever it is. Let's get this over with.*

"All weekend," she continued, "I have been asking God, 'What is it about Angela? Why have we all fallen in love with Angela?'"

I sat there, searching her eyes for some kind of clue about where this was going. I couldn't imagine what in the world she was getting ready to say.

"Angela, I believe we have all fallen in love with you . . . because you're so . . . ordinary."

Even now, I smile as I remember her honesty. That was the deepest, truest encouragement I have ever known. I don't think Aldyth could have paid me a higher compliment, because in those few words she spoke, she may as well have said this: *God, in His divine wisdom, decided that an ordinary woman, who lives in Tennessee, should pack her ordinary bags and put on her ordinary jeans and style her ordinary hair and grab her ordinary friend and drive her ordinary car to the airport to fly an ordinary plane to go and tell some ordinary women her stories about ordinary hurt and ordinary disappointment and ordinary brokenness. But when an ordinary, broken-down woman has laid herself on the altar of God, He stoops down in His mercy. He comes running with compassion. And every time an ordinary woman lays her truth on God's altar, He promises to raise her up, made extraordinary by His healing and His redemption and His mercy and His unfailing, extravagant love.*

Maybe this morning you woke up in your ordinary bed and rolled over to look at an ordinary pillow where no ordinary man sleeps. You walked into your ordinary bathroom and stared at that ordinary woman with the ordinary puffiness underneath her ordinary eyes. You put on your ordinary clothes and made an ordinary breakfast, kissed your ordinary kids, and drove in your ordinary car to their ordinary school. Hurried to your ordinary desk at your ordinary job with those ordinary people and their ordinary excuses. Then looked up to heaven and heard your broken heart cry, *What in the world will God ever do with an ordinary woman like me?*

Maybe, right this minute, you need to hear God's voice saying to you, *Hey, you with the heavy load. Lay it down. Just put it all right here in front of Me. All your dreams and your insecurities and your pain. Everything those kids want you to be. All your worry and the responsibilities that are too much for one woman to bear. The disappointment over how life turned out. Your weakness and your weariness and your aching body. The constant needs that never go away and the little battles that just rip out your joy. Lay it down and come to Me. Come in your ordinary. It's OK. I do extraordinary work with ordinary women like you. These circumstances will not win. Love has the final say.*

my love lessons

LOVE HEALS. A few years after the divorce, one of my children began to cry a lot, get angry, hit people, and stomp away to the bedroom. As soon as I figured out that my kid was hurting and not just being plain mean, I took that child to a counselor, asking, "Why now? Why not in the beginning? Why has all this time passed, and *now* my baby's acting mad?" The counselor told me that this particular child is a "stuffer." A stuffer pretends to be OK. Hides the tears. Lies about the pain. Smiles to make both parents happy. But eventually the stuffer gets full, as mine did, and all that has been pushed down comes out. Anger. Deep sadness. Frustration.

So I kept taking the "overstuffed" child to the counselor, who cost ninety bucks an hour, so she could take a crowbar to my child's heart and force the full one to spill melancholy guts all over the place. I kept thinking, *If that kid could just throw up, well, that would just feel better.* The sweet, kind, tenderhearted counselor would always *tell* me she'd had a great session with my kid—except my stuffer would never speak. No words. No sharing. Nothing. Just more keeping it in and feeling sick. The thing that was supposed to help my hurting kid just left us looking at each other.

Finally, after several weeks of go-nowhere counseling, I decided to stop what wasn't working on this kid and save my ninety bucks.

But I still didn't know what to do.

Eventually, not exactly out of wisdom, but because there was nothing else to try, I sat the stuffed-up, teary-eyed, freshly-punished-for-another-outburst-of-anger kid down for a lesson on love. It went a little like this:

"You have every reason to be mad at me. At the rest of the family. At every person who breathes," I said. "And I have never been a kid with divorced parents, so I'm sure I have no idea what kind of pain you are keeping inside. I get it. I totally get why you'd be mad. It makes sense to me. But even though I get it, there are a couple of things I cannot allow.

"I can't allow you to hit anyone in your anger. You will have to use your words and tell the truth and tell me or someone else what is going on inside of you.

"I also won't allow you to stay like this. I cannot let you begin to find comfort in bitterness. Life doesn't go like you planned sometimes. None of the people who live on this planet are exempt from heartache or disappointment. What matters is what you do with what has come to you. Bitterness will keep you locked in a cage for the rest of your life. I won't allow a child of mine to think like that or act like that. Besides, you look so pitiful there inside that cage.

"Baby, look at me. Here is my promise to you. My love for you is without end. I am totally, unashamedly, and wildly in love with you. Your dad is crazy in love with you. I am not going anywhere. I am for you and I believe in you, and a really bad attitude or even a really bad day isn't going to change how I feel about you. You live inside this family, and our love is strong. I am going to be on your team for the rest of your life. Every time you show up or stand up and just get your cute, little body up out of that bed, I will be cheering for you like one of those embarrassing wack-a-doo moms in the stands.

"We're going to get through this sad place, and we're going to get through every other thing that comes to us. I am your mom. I'm not scared of hard. Or afraid to do whatever it takes to love you well. I love you, honey. It's all going to be OK. You are going to be an amazing person, with the biggest heart of compassion. God's gonna use that heart of yours to take care of people all over the world. I can't wait to see what great, big things He does with you."

And do you know what happened after that big I'm-gonna-love-you-no-matter-what talk? My stuffed kid woke up a little different the next day. So I just leaned in with more love and told the other kids to give the grumpy one a break. When the sad one would walk by, I'd say something like, "When you smile like that, it takes up the whole kitchen." And the next day was a little easier. With a little more consistent, keep-it-going love, my angry kid was downright mellow and happy.

I believe love healed that kid. Just like love is healing me. I'm learning that love has the final say about things like pain. You can read great books on healing techniques and take advantage of months of necessary counseling. All wonderful tools, but when love kicks in, watch out! Somebody is going to get healed.

LOVE MADE ME SURRENDER. When my first two children were born, I was sure that I was going to be an amazing mom. I probably could have won some kind of award in my town for packing the best ready-for-any-disaster diaper bag. I dressed those first two in identical outfits, with little monogrammed collars, and then coordinated myself to go with the matching babes. They always held my hand and obeyed when I spoke, and they ate healthy food and took a two-hour nap every afternoon. I signed them up for enlightening activities and took them to every playland experience within a hundred miles. In those first baby years, I was fairly proud of myself and my supermom abilities. And I'm sure my excessive (and repulsive) behavior was borderline intolerable to everyone else. A striving woman is not attractive. I was a striving mom.

Never mind that I had stressed myself right into the outer realm of oblivion by the ridiculous expectations I had placed on myself and the kids. I was determined that they would have the best preschools and the best teachers and know more about God than any five-year-old can comprehend, and eventually they would become the best surgeons and attorneys and serve impoverished children all over the world.

Living and loving my children as a single mom has done something almost miraculous for me. I became so overwhelmed with providing for four that I had to give up trying to make them into perfect little people. I am learning to see who they are and how they came wired and just let them unfold themselves. Their individual quirks and fascinating personalities are like undiscovered treasure. It has been huge for me to let them like what they like and then enjoy it with them.

Grayson and William just called. They just got back from the coolest skate park ever while visiting their dad. Just so you know, if I had been choosing an activity for my boys, I am sure I would have never chosen skateboarding. But they absolutely love it. They spend their money on custom boards and bearings and grip tape and stupid, expensive shoes. They are eaten up with skateboarding.

"Today was awesome, Mom! You should have been there. They have a half-pipe and ramps and huge drop-ins and rails—"

"Wow, honey! That sounds like the best time ever. Were you scared on the drop-ins?"

"Yeah, but we loved it. They have a balcony where parents can come and watch. Mom, you have to come."

"I can't wait. I'll pray while you scare the spit out of me."

Giggle, giggle. "Cool."

My boys think they're going to be professional skateboarders and they'll make a lot of money to take care of their families with all the sponsorships they will get from skateboard manufacturers and sports drinks and bubble gum and stuff like that. About five years ago, the prospect of skateboard professionals in the family would have driven me nuts. I would have taken every opportunity to correct their immature thinking and skater-dude logic. I would have probably broken their hearts as well.

My kids go to a school with uniforms and a dress code. I love that. It's the best thing ever that my four kids don't have to think about what to wear in the mornings. Our hardest part is everybody remembering to grab a belt on the way out the door. Other than that, I think uniforms rock. But we do have a hair issue. The school wants it neat, and skateboard guys like it big and fluffy. Grayson is all about his hair right now, and the neat thing is cramping his style. The old mom in me would have been a rule keeper, maybe even stricter than the school. The mom who is being changed by love found out it's just hair. So I tell him, "Grayson, we have to obey the rules. The school has a rule about hair, and it's important to respect their authority. But how about this: you can grow your hair right up to the line of their dress code." He thinks I'm being cool. I know I'm just giving in to love.

I expect my boys probably won't be professional skateboarders, but love is teaching me how to surrender. To see past the little things and care more about their hearts. I have good boys—I do know that—and even if they kick-flip their shaggy-headed selves through life, they will still be good boys with good hearts who just happen to skateboard for a living.

Being a single mom who is learning how to love better has taken the edge off of me. They probably won't graduate from Harvard, but I hope they're smart in the things they care about and laugh a lot and wear funky clothes and listen to God more than suffering to live up to some stupid, mom-imposed standard.

Love made me surrender, and the heavy weight of over-achieving has been lifted.

LOVE COVERS ALL KIND OF FLAWS. My kids, God bless them, were given a very imperfect mom. Besides never mastering the crafty thing, I have so much more that comes up short. I can't swim so great, so I'm a little hyperparanoid around water. I can't keep my eyes open after ten, so that keeps me from being the cool parent who takes her kids for doughnuts around midnight. I don't like messiness; therefore, messy things, like paint or homemade slime or papier-mâché, have to stay outside, preferably down the street, at the neighbor's house. I work puzzles but have little patience for board games. I never watch TV, so I don't get it when they are quoting some new commercial from the cartoon channel. I have more, but I will spare you the three-volume set on my flawed nature.

What I want you to know is that, in some divine way, love covers for me. And love just keeps winning. The kids are drawn in, and our home is happy and blessed and functioning. And the reason it's working just has to be love.

LOVE MAKES YOU FORGET. There is a weird thing about the feminine soul. We are inherently able to remember all the times we've been done wrong by a man. By whom we have been hurt. The gory details. And, given just a minute, what we were wearing. It is a heavy burden to carry around such a finely tuned memory. Forgiveness takes so much longer when you can't disconnect yourself from the minutiae of being offended.

But love, love seems to have an eraser. When you focus more on extending love than keeping a record of offenses, it rubs out the occasional transgression. So, build love. Plant tiny love seeds in the hearts of little people who look like you. When you set your intent on love, practice love, read about love, and become *changed* by love, painful memories begin to fade.

When love takes over, you don't have time for grudges anymore. Love has bigger things to do. Adventures to live. Kids to grow. It probably sounds unbelievable, but I can't remember very much of the past five years. Don't get me wrong; there are accumulated hurts. If I stopped and tried, I could begin to recount who has done me wrong. But it doesn't matter. Love is growing me up and over.

GOD'S LOVE RESCUES AND PROTECTS THE ONES WHO CALL ON HIS NAME. It is one thing to say such a spiritual thing and an entirely different thing to experience it. I have been the woman tied to the tracks of an oncoming train. I have been without any clear path or means to save myself. I have been in desperate need of a hero.

People ask me all the time, "How in the world have you done this? How did you go from zero to hope?" The truth is, I have been rescued by the love of God.

When I had no idea who to trust, I called on God.

When I didn't have money to pay the rent, I pleaded with God.

When I thought my kids might be crushed, I cried out to God.

When I was afraid of accusers, I ran to God.

God *will* come to rescue and protect you and your children. Maybe you have been everywhere else. Maybe you have tried in your own strength. All I know for sure is, "Trust God." Trust that every promise He has made to you is true. I know you may not feel ready to trust anyone yet, but I'm urging you to go ahead and live like you trust Him. Talk like you trust Him. Lay your head on your pillow at night and sleep like you trust Him.

What else do we have? I have no one else in heaven or on earth who could care for me like this. God's consistency has been astounding to everyone who knows me. I remember telling my attorney many times, "We are going to walk this out with God." I don't think they teach that in law school, but he was gracious and just let me babble on about trusting God to protect me. My attorney took my instruction about the high road and choosing to follow the wisdom taught in the book of Proverbs. I'm sure he had plenty of doubt along the way. In fact, I bet there were days when he thought I needed to lay down the Jesus talk. But today I think he would tell you he can't believe how good God has been the children and me.

So many incredibly unfair things have come our way, but God has this restoration principle that just keeps coming through for us time after time. In the book of Joel, God speaks through the prophet and says to me and to you, "*I will repay you for the years the locusts have eaten*" (2:25 NIV). My counselor has spoken that passage over me many times. I can't tell you how many people have prayed those very words for me. And the most compelling truth I have to tell you is that God *is* repaying us. It feels as though whole years of my life have been eaten by locusts. But what the locusts have eaten in my life, God is making good on His promise to give back. Multiplied.

It makes me mad all the time that we still have to battle evil and foolishness. And a fallen world means there will be more to come. But I will do all I know to do and call on the love of God. And then rest.

WHERE THERE IS LOVE, EVENTUALLY THERE IS HOPE. In the beginning of my single-mom life, I don't think I had very much hope, but I did have an undying "momma love" for my children. You know that kind of love: the one that gets you through a couple of years where you can't remember how anybody got fed. But lo and behold, they have all eaten, every single day, because love stood you up and drove you to the grocery store and pulled you through.

It's the kind of love that keeps you playing UNO every night before bedtime, when all you can see are colors, because you're so exhausted. The kind that sends you from bed to bed to scratch the backs of sleepy kids, even while your heart aches for someone to put his hand in the center of *your* back and rub gently until *you* fall asleep.

Momma love is the love that was born inside of us the very day our first newborn took a breath.

It was this love that made me decide that my children deserved a mom who was excited about being alive. Looking for good in them and in us and in the circumstances we encounter. Resisting self-pity. Forgiving and then acting like forgiveness really forgives. Believing in the dark. Standing up when I just want to fall down. Acting brave because I believe God. I believe He really loves us. And I believe love always wins.

I haven't a clue what lies ahead for the children and me. I imagine there will still be pain and unpleasant surprises and more battles to fight. But the one thing that keeps renewing my faith is my love for them and God's love for all of us. And where there is love, eventually hope comes into view.

LOVE ROLLS AWAY THE STONE. Today is Good Friday. I know why they call it that, but honestly, today has felt more like sad Friday or black Friday. I've been thinking about Jesus all day long. Today the whole world marks the sacrifice He made. The passion of our Christ. The cross. His death. The mourning and grief as we remember our Messiah: beaten, pierced, and hung on a cross to pay a penalty He never deserved. The Bible says the sun stopped shining when Jesus died. The sky was torn. All creation cried.

This afternoon my thoughts have turned to the ones who

loved Jesus. The disciples. His mother. The others who had followed Him into Jerusalem that Palm Sunday. Can you imagine what it felt like for them to watch their Hope being placed inside a tomb and a stone rolled over the entrance? They must have walked home that dark night devastated. Empty. Inconsolable and filled with desperate, unbearable grief. I'm sure there was no reprieve for the deep sorrow they knew.

It surely felt as if all was lost. Nothing could have mattered to them after Jesus died. He had been their very lives and their hope for the future, and that day, Friday, He was gone.

I took a walk just now and began to think about the wait. A stone over a grave. The Savior inside. All of the kingdom of heaven on earth waiting. Holding its holy breath. Mustering a righteous patience. Aching with anticipation for what was yet to be. Waiting for the power of the Resurrection.

Dear single mom, has a stone been rolled over the tomb that contains your hope? Does your heart feel dead? Do you grieve or mourn with a desperate sadness? I ask you to wait. Wait a holy wait for the promised resurrection. Wait for God to send angels to roll away the stone. Wait in righteousness. Wait in your grief. Wait with anticipation. He is coming. The Lord is risen indeed, and His promised power will come to take away your sorrow.

I will wait with you at the tomb of our heartache. Jesus is alive, and He is the One who will save us now and for all eternity. And He is coming with the full power of His resurrection. He will wipe away every tear and restore every hope, some on this earth and all promised for eternity. Let us wait with anticipation. Let us set our affection on Him. Let us love our children well. Love will roll away this stone, and love will have the final say.

● ● ●

At the beginning of this book, I told you I am absolutely sure this is not how it's supposed to be. Single mom. Houseful o' kids. Broken life. Wounded hearts. Slugging along. Lots of missteps. A few great steps. I am still sure that kids should be raised with two parents who love each other. But some days I wonder . . . I wonder if I'm a better woman because of all this struggle. I wonder if the kids are going to be stronger because of what we've been through together. I wonder if we'll all love deeper and embrace blessings sooner because we know what it feels like to live alone and afraid.

I'm just wondering if what you once thought of as awful can become the best thing that ever happened. When life takes a turn you never expected, suddenly you are on a road not marked on any map. It's the scariest, thorniest, most treacherous road you've ever walked. And then, one day, around a corner, it's the most beautiful place you've ever been. What if being a single mom is like that? One day the pain is covered over by love, and what has been awful turns into the best life you've ever known.

Do you remember the words of Joseph back in the Old Testament? He said to his brothers, "As far as I am concerned, God turned into good what you meant for evil" (Gen. 50:20 NLT).

And then there are the words of the apostle Paul to the church in Rome: "And we know that in all things God works for the good of those who love him (Rom. 8:28 NIV).

That's the kind of thing God likes to do. He works terrible things out for good. He loves to take circumstances like ours and make breathtaking, God-glorifying good come from it.

Maybe you woke up this morning to your everyday life. And the same kids you had yesterday. And your regular problems with regular bills and the regular seemingly no way out. Maybe it's even worse than usual, and evil met you for breakfast, with another attack that makes you feel desperate and alone. Maybe you wonder what in the world God can do with an ordinary single mom and her ordinary, run-of-the-mill kids. I am believing for both of us that the Bible is true.

I believe God will restore to you what has been taken.

I believe He will bring good from all the difficult things that have come to you.

I believe He will come to your rescue and protect you and your children from harm.

I believe He has a hope and a future for you that is beyond anything you can dream for yourself.

I believe God's love can heal you and your children, better than new.

I believe He can cover every place in which you feel inadequate and make you enough.

I believe doing all that you can is all God requires.

I believe wayward kids can come home. And
broken hearts can be mended.

I believe His forgiveness really forgives.

I believe God's grace to moms is lavish and gentle.

I believe it's time to dream again. And laugh more.
And be silly for a change.

I believe our kids are going to turn out great because
they are His. And He loves them more than we
know how to love.

I believe there will be more disappointment, but we
are stronger and wiser and more prepared to act
like a grown-up.

I believe an ordinary woman becomes extraordinary in
the arms of God.

I believe your soul can rest. We live inside the
kingdom of God, and He totally knows
what to do. And here's what He has to
say about you:

> *I have loved you with an everlasting love.*
> (Jer. 31:3 NIV)

But from everlasting to everlasting
  the Lord's love is with those who fear him,
  and his righteousness with their children's children.
(Ps. 103:17 NIV)

Yep, no doubt about it. Love has the final say.

about the author

Angela Thomas is a mother of four, a dynamic speaker, and an author of ten books and Bible studies, including the best-selling book, *Do You Think I'm Beautiful?* Speaking from her own brokenness and God's great love, Angela motivates us all to live faithful, passionate lives. She teaches at numerous events every year where women all around the world are drawn to her warmth, wit, and vulnerability. Angela and her children live on a really great street in Knoxville, Tennessee, close to family and surrounded by some of the best people on the planet.

acknowledgments

For a couple of years I have joked with my family and friends that I'm going to have a t-shirt made. I decided that the shirt should read, "When I get the book done." And then when someone needed something or wanted to know when we were going to have home-cooked meals or learn to snowboard or go to Disney World, then all I would have to do is point to the t-shirt instead of wearing us all out by saying the same old thing all the time.

This past Christmas, my oldest daughter, Taylor, sat on the edge of her chair watching me open the gift she had chosen for me. Turns out that my creative one had made the t-shirt. A white, long-sleeve number with beautiful lettering that reads, When I get the book done. I have worn that sweet gift with great pride. And I am thrilled to announce to the whole family . . . What do you know, the book is done!

Thank you Grayson, Taylor, William and AnnaGrace. Really and truly, you are the most amazing kids on the planet. We had such a fun summer traveling after the book was done. I want you to know that I'd rather be with you than anybody. Thank you for putting up with my travel and the deadlines and the house renovation and the all-in-all craziness that goes along with being in our family. I love you more than anything in this world and I would give up everything times a million just to have you as my children.

Thank you to Lisa Stridde, her husband Dave and the kids who put up with their mama and me, Jordan, Morgan and Tyler. There is just no way my family would make it without you in our lives.

Thank you to the other family who thinks we belong to their family, Greg and Kim Shelton, Parker and Bailey. None of us can eat a hot Krispy Kreme without thinking about you and how much fun we all have being together.

Thank you to my mom and dad, my brothers and their families, my Texas family and my Tulsa brother. Your love holds me up, and you know I'd be lost without you.

Thank you my dear friends, Dennis and Karen Larkin, Laura Johnson, Roy and Nicole Newman, Lou Taylor, Lee and Carla Martin, Brad and Beth Brinson, Cindy Millikan, Paul Kelly and my friend, Scott, for every pep talk you have given to me and every tear you have caught in your hands.

Thank you to my girlfriends who are doing what I do every weekend too, Lisa Whelchel, Priscilla Shirer and Kim Hill. Your prayers, texts and calls make the shared journey very beautiful.

Thank you Martha Judiscak for caring about this book with your research and prayers.

What is always amazing to me is that God continues to

send the most loving people to take care of me and the children. Thank you Two Rivers Church, Mike Turner, Dave Benner, Sid Kemp, Clayton and Elaine Bryant, Beverly Wallace, Jeff and Tammy Smith and a very huge thanks to all the people who faithfully pray for my family and my work.

Thank you Aldyth and Cathy. I love you both and cannot wait until we're together again.

Thank you to my friends at Thomas Nelson, Mike Hyatt, Tami Heim, Jonathan Merkh and Brian Hampton. I can't think of anything better than working with people you really like and admire. I am grateful to be one of the kids in your family.

Thank you to LifeWay, World Vision, the radio stations around the country who have let me talk between their music and most especially, thank you to Creative Trust, David Huffman, Jessica Wolstenholm, Jim Houser, Dan Raines, Jeanie Kaserman and Jenny Stika. Wow, look at what God has done!

Every single day I am overwhelmed by the goodness of God. The end of this book is no different. That the Lord God Almighty would choose me to give a message of His love and faithfulness is both humbling and awesome. I love what I get to do and grin from ear to ear all the time because of it. But I am intimately aware of where these gifts come from. Every good and perfect gift comes directly from the hands of my Father. I pray that my life and these words will bring glory to the Giver and that the intent of my heart will bless His name forever and ever.

Other titles from

ANGELA THOMAS

DO YOU THINK I'M BEAUTIFUL
ISBN 0-7852-6355-1 | $19.99
ISBN 0-7852-7377-8 (trade paper) | $13.99

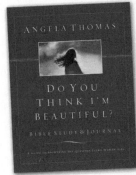

**DO YOU THINK I'M BEAUTIFUL
BIBLE STUDY**
ISBN 0-7852-6223-7 | $17.99

A BEAUTIFUL OFFERING
ISBN 0-7852-6357-8 | $19.99

**BEAUTIFUL OFFERING BIBLE
STUDY DVD**
ISBN 1-4158-2092-9 | $149.95